PASSION P

PEACE

The Pathway through Trials and Tribulations

Visionary Author Dr. Theresa A. Moseley
Foreword By Melissa Love
Afterword Author Dr. Desziree Richardson

©2022 by Dr. Theresa A. Moseley

Cover Copyright © 2022 Dr. Theresa A. Moseley

All rights reserved. Except as permitted under U.S. Copyright Act of 1976, no part of this publication may be reproduced, distributed, or transmitted in any form or by any means, or stored in a database or retrieval system, without the prior written permission of the publisher, except in cases of brief quotation embodied in the critical reviews and specific non-commercial uses permitted by copyright law.

The scanning, uploading, and distribution of this book without permission is a theft of the author's intellectual property. If you would like permission to use material from the book (other than for review purposes), please contact TAM Creating Ambassadors of Peace. Thank you for your support and author's rights.

Published by Dr. Theresa A. Moseley September 2, 2022

Address: Upper Marlboro, Maryland
Website: www.creatingambassadorsofpeace.com
Email: theresaamoseley2@gmail.com
Phone Number:443 228 8827
Facebook: Dr. Theresa A. Moseley

Printed in the United States of America

ISBN 979-8-9865003-0-0

Acknowledgments

I thank God for giving me guidance every day to live out my divine assignment. Every morning when I pray, I ask God to guide me in the right direction to fulfill my mission in life. I realized my divine assignment was to help and serve others to fulfill their purpose and create inner peace. This book will serve as a tool to help others realize that no matter how bad things are, there is a light at the end of the tunnel.

I am thankful for my amazing children, Maria, Melissa, Nadia, and Anna, who continue to support me during all my book projects. Melissa was so gracious to accept my offer to write the foreword for this book. Her insight into the stories of my contributing authors is outstanding. I want to thank Dr. Tasheka L. Green for mentoring me through this process of publishing my first anthology. She has been a great resource and friend through this process. Thank you Dr. Desziree Richardson for your willingness to write the afterword for this book. Your insight into the author's stories was on point. You are a jewel and I appreciate you.

Roland Pollard Sr., thank you for the music to my song "Passion Purpose Peace." As I wrote the lyrics, I had no idea how the wonderful music you created to go with the melody would be so uplifting. You are an amazing composer and I pray it becomes an anthem for peace. A special thanks to Dr. Rhonda M. Wood who has stood by my side through my trials and tribulations this year. She has been the best sister a friend can have. Finally, a special thanks to all my contributing authors for the time and effort in developing your chapters. I could not have done this without you. I know this book will impact the world as your powerful messages of hope, will, faith, perseverance, and resilience will have a positive impact on someone in need of guidance to find inner peace.

Dedication

I dedicate this book to my dad, the late S. F. C. Clarence B. Moseley, whose last words to me were, “Go live in your purpose.” I also dedicate this book to my cousins Pat and LaVance, and my two students who died from violence, Brandon and Israel. I will NEVER forget you.

Table of Contents

Introduction

DR. THERESA A. MOSELEY

"Not everyone will be happy when you begin to better yourself. Those who are for you will not just celebrate in your triumphs, but they will also pray with you through your tribulations."

T. D. Jakes

The quote by Bishop T.D. Jakes best describes my relationships with the contributing authors in this book. They have celebrated my success and they have been there for me during my tribulations. During the last two years, I lost relatives to Covid, Parkinson's disease, and cancer. I did not have to grieve alone as these friends showed up and helped me heal my wounded heart. Also, during this time, the violence in our nation increased. It seemed like every time I turned on the news or picked up my phone, there was another mass shooting. As an educator, it really hits hard to hear about children dying in school during a mass shooting. I know what that feels like to lose a student or family member to gun violence. I experienced the death of two students killed one year apart. One was shot to death and the other was beaten to death. This started my campaign for No More Violence. I know that the message I was sending in the community was needed around the world. I began to speak and write my messages on world peace.

Sometimes you meet people for a season and sometimes for a reason. There was a reason why I met every contributing author in this anthology.

This project was meant to be completed with this team of authors. Their journeys are similar, the trials and tribulations are often the same, and their journey to find their truth as Miriam so eloquently states, “take off the mask,” will help others find their pathway to inner peace. The authors begin with quotes, some biblical, some created by the author, and others by prominent people. The quotes are aligned with their content, and they share stories of their journey to inner peace.

Foreword

MELISSA LOVE

"I have told you these things, so that in me you may have peace. In this world, you will have trouble. But take heart! I have overcome the world." John 16:33

The human body is an amazing creation. When injured or damaged the body has the incredible capacity to heal itself. Our bodies are designed to fight off infection, heal wounds, repair damaged body parts, fight the aging process, and much more. Remember falling off your bike as a child and scraping your knee on the ground? Seeing the white meat, bleeding, and feeling the stinging sensation immediately brought tears to your eyes. Perhaps you were told to throw some dirt on it and keep it moving or maybe someone gently comforted you, treated your wound with loving care, and gave you a popsicle before sending you back outside to play. A few days later a scab would appear and within a week or two, your knee was as good as new until the next fateful fall.

John 16:33 says, "In this world, you will have trouble." This is a guarantee. You WILL have trouble because we live in a fallen world with broken people and broken systems. Therefore, pain is inevitable. Every person in their life experiences physical and emotional pain or trauma. The same way others responded differently to our boo-boos as children, we also have a choice as to how we respond to the pain we endure. We respond to our pain by ignoring or pretending that the hurt isn't there. We pacify our pain with substances, material possessions, and even success. We fall into depression and anxiety. We take our pain out on the people who are closest to us. There are many ways that we respond to pain but many of these responses keep us hurt and hurting, not healing.

I love the story of Joseph in the Bible. Son of Jacob, he was despised by his brothers who planned to kill him but ended up selling him into slavery instead. While enslaved in Egypt he was falsely accused and imprisoned, but he continued to allow God to use him no matter his circumstances. Eventually, because of his devotion to God and the gifts that God empowered him with, he was raised to a high position in the land and ultimately saved his family who abandoned him and left him for dead. When Joseph finally confronted his brothers, he told them, "You intended to harm me, but God intended it for good to accomplish what is now being done, the saving of many lives." Joseph turned his pain into purpose and saved his family and the entire land of Canaan from famine. Forgiveness and reconciliation took place and Joseph and his entire family lived peacefully together in Egypt for generations.

The stories in this book include brave people who share some of their most painful experiences. Each storyteller is as unique as their source or sources of pain. However, what they have in common is like Joseph, they decided not to become a prisoner of pain. Instead, each person pursued a journey toward healing that turned their pain into purpose and ultimately allowed them to experience inner peace. These contributors share practical steps that we can implement in our lives as we journey from wounded to heal. We weren't created to live as wounded, broken people. We were created to be image bearers, that is our ultimate purpose. By the grace of God, it will be done because He HAS overcome the world and peace is yours right now if you only receive it.

Melissa Love is a wife to USAF Col. (retired) Antonio Love and a proud mother of six children. Melissa is a graduate of the University of Maryland and has a degree in Psychology. She is the Program Coordinator for The NOMORE Foundation, a non-profit organization that seeks to help connect the local church to the most vulnerable in their communities. Melissa is a seminary student at Asbury Theological Seminary pursuing a Master of Divinity. She is a preacher, prayer warrior, Spirit-led leader, and a proud member of Jack and Jill of America, Inc., where she serves as Chaplain in the Greater Tampa Chapter. Melissa is also co-editor and contributing author of *The Gospel in Full Color* (2020), a daily devotional that focuses on the Bible's call for justice, reconciliation, and the beauty of diversity.

Facebook: Melissa Love

Instagram: melissamialove

No Passion, No Purpose, No Peace
Know Passion, Know Purpose, Know Peace

Dr. Tasheka L. Green

"Where there is passion, there is purpose. Where there is purpose, there is peace. Where there is peace, there is your reward."

Know Passion

Passion: A powerful emotion, such as love and joy, ardent love, and boundless enthusiasm.

Passion motivates you to your purpose. You should always let your passion be the reason for your purpose. Passion is what pushes you to a place where you never give up or give in. What you are passionate about, you did not choose; it chose you. Your passion was created in you; it is not by the circumstance that you have a burning desire for something that gives you joy. Your passion is your purpose: what you are committed to and wake up every morning to pursue.

When you let your passion be your purpose, you will understand what living is about. This type of passion is the fire that lights the way to the journey of your purpose. When you exhibit this passion, it is demonstrated through compassion, and an abundance of peace will overtake you.

My mother's death was painful and one of the lowest points in my life. However, my pain during the process birthed purpose, healing, inspiration, motivation, and life for someone else. My passion for inspiring others amid their trials and suffering led to my purpose. Passion and purpose collaborated to produce the plan of God for my life. You cannot have passion without purpose, and you cannot have purpose without passion.

When you have passion and you are walking in your purpose, you have peace, and peace is your reward. The reward that you are seeking is within you. It is the peace you desire and the peace you seek. You do not have to look for it; lean into it. Peace is a choice, and the peace you seek is on the inside of you. Peace begins with you. This peace means embracing who you are and walking in the steps God has ordered. "Peace, I leave with you; my peace I give you. I do not give to you as the world gives. Do not let your hearts be troubled and do not be afraid" (John 14:27, NIV).

Know Purpose

Purpose: The reason something is done or created or for which something exists.

"And we know that in all things God works for the good of those who love him, who have been called according to his purpose" (Romans 8:28, NIV). All that I have been through, God approved it, allowed it, and made it complete to summon me to his purpose for my life.

On one side, my purpose was birthed through a process of pain; on the other, my purpose was birthed through passion. In life, we go through tests and trials that seem to make the best out of our lives. We cry, scream, pull, and try to hibernate from the hurt and humiliation. We face challenges in our homes, marriages, families, children, jobs, finances, health, the death of loved ones, and the list could go on. These afflictions tend to weigh us down, get us off course, and magnify a fictitious image that we will not fulfill our purpose. "Many are the afflictions of the righteous: but the Lord delivered him out of them all" (Psalms 34:19, KJV).

My purpose was birthed out of pain because my mother's death triggered life for my purpose. I had to trust the process through the pain, knowing that I would birth a purpose that was sealed with passion.

When I was eliminated from an executive-level position in 2018, not only did I have to activate faith, but also, I had to agree with it as well for me to move from the old and step into the new. I had to see things from a new lens and surrender what was predictable and comfortable.

I had to step into the unknown, uncharted territories and embrace the favor that greeted me. I had to wait and watch with joyous expectations and see the accomplished work. I had to stand in the strength of God's promises and disallow anyone else to take the glory. I could not allow the fear of failure and the voices of accusation to cripple and hinder me from moving forward. I had to shake off discouragement, let go of despair, and relinquish to God's plan, promise, and purpose.

Most of all, I had to forgive those who mistreated me and surrender my right to hold a grudge. I had to let God's peace be greater than my understanding. I had to listen with a voice of peace and declare with faith, confidence, and courage to manifest the purpose of God. The door that abruptly closed in 2018 was an opportunity for the windows of heaven to open and pour out a blessing. The same area that seemed like a struggle or challenge has become my greatest strength. I had to overcome doubt in my life and stretch my faith until it was greater than the weight I carried to execute the next assignment.

As I reflect, celebrate, and rejoice, I am grateful for all the Lord has done because God remembered Tasheka. Nevertheless, it was not until I was at peace with myself, others, and the matters that surrounded me, that I could truly embrace the passion and walk in my purpose.

Although I was eliminated in 2018, this process started in 2010 when my mom passed away. My mom's death brought forth life for me; it brought forth purpose. It took my ordinary and turned it into extraordinary. It allowed me to start a business, a memorial scholarship foundation, and a women's award to celebrate her legacy. In 2010, when all of this commenced, only God knew what would take place in 2018 and allowed me to walk right into what He had already prepared for me.

Be driven by the passion that leads you to your purpose because purpose can never be interrupted. Remember, when you passionately walk in your purpose, you never have to chase opportunities; they will come looking for you.

Know Peace

Peace: A state of tranquility or quiet; freedom from disquieting or oppressive thoughts or emotions.

I consciously chose to lean into peace, stay committed to it, and follow the path that God was leading. I had to let go of worry because the worry was too much to bear. I had to bring order to chaos because the chaos was too much to maneuver through. I had to loosen the grip of doubt, unrelenting distractions, and discouragement, and focus on what was promised. I had to focus on my peace. Peace is my companion.

When you make up in your mind to choose peace, God will begin to expose those people in your life whose intentions were not after the heart of God for your life. God will remove them and surround you with people who are committed to your success. They will guard your secrets and cover your weaknesses. They will never bruise your spirit or scar your soul. They will love you to victory and celebrate your passion and purpose. Be encouraged and know that your work and labor of love are not in vain. Keep doing what is right because it is the right thing to do. Love without an agenda or an expectation of something in return and stay focused on your peace.

Did you know that you were not just created for labor, but you were created for rest, to be at peace and in peace? You were created to be in tranquility and a place of freedom from disquieting or oppressive thoughts or emotions. You were not created to collapse under weight or pressure. You were created to be more than a conqueror. You will find the entire fulfillment you need in a place called rest, a place of peace.

The cares of life can clutter your thoughts and fog your vision, but only if you allow them to. Keep your mind on the peace that was given to you and disallow the noise to interrupt the sound of quietness. You will never clearly hear the instructions for the purpose and assignment for your life until you find your place of peace. You will find answers, productivity, and strength in the quietness and stillness.

Peace is invaluable, priceless. It cannot be compromised. Peace is more precious than any stone. Peace is the protection you need to guard your heart and mind. Always let God's peace be greater than your understanding. "And the peace of God, which transcends all understanding, will guard your hearts and your minds in Christ Jesus" (Philippians 4:7, NIV).

Peace Is Your Reward

Reward: Something of value given in return for an act, a prize promised for a certain deed.

Your reward is peace when you are driven by passion and walking in your purpose. Consider some women of the bible who were driven by passion, walked in purpose, and were rewarded with the peace of God. Ruth's husband Boaz had died, and she was in an unfamiliar place as a foreign woman in a Jewish land. Ruth had lost her husband, but she knew there was purpose in her, a promise, and a reward waiting for her. She was committed to her promise and submitted herself to Naomi. She remained loyal to Naomi and was led by her heart and not her head. She knew that Naomi had what she needed to get her to where she needed to be. But God remembered Ruth, and through the eyes of Boaz, he acknowledged her and said, "Now, my dear, don't worry! I intend to do for you everything you propose, for everyone in the village knows that you are a worthy woman" (Ruth 3:11, NET). Ruth conceived a child, and God used her in the lineage of His Son, Jesus.

Hannah, barren Hannah, could not conceive and was the first of two wives of Elkanah. Hannah, whose name meant grace and favor. Hannah had the gift of intercession. Hannah was taunted and teased by Peninnah. But God remembered Hannah, and she gave birth to Samuel (asked of God).

Samuel was a great prophet of the Old Testament. He was a bridge, a connecting link, between the patriarchs, judges, and kings. Samuel grew up to reflect his mother's love for God.

Esther, whose name meant hidden, was born with the name Hadassah. When Esther was young, she lost her parents and became an orphan. She was a Jewish woman who radiated with beauty in the presence of a foreign King. But God remembered Esther, and she became the Queen. Esther had passion and purpose and was at peace with her decision to lead the Jews and yield to God's purpose for her life. She followed God's plan, walked in purpose, and rescued the Jewish nation.

Moreover, we cannot forget Sarah, at 90 years old, gave birth to the promise, Isaac, meaning the one who laughs. Remember Sarah, who laughed behind the door when God said she would give birth to a child. God caught Sarah laughing and said, "Is anything too hard for God." But God remembered Sarah. Hebrews 11:11 (NIV) tells us that by faith, even Sarah, who was past childbearing age, was enabled to bear children because she considered him faithful who had made the promise. It does not matter who you are, what you have done, where you are from, the mistakes you have made, or how old you are; if you are still here, go and live a life full of passion and purpose. Leverage everything inside of you, your calling, gift, passion, and purpose, to be whom God says.

Sometimes we are waiting for a revelation, a prophecy, an epiphany, or something to drop in our laps when God is waiting for us to leverage everything in us to draw us closer to where we are supposed to be. He sees you as a finished work.

Your gifts will make room for you and bring you before great men. God has already made way and set you up for the world to see how good He is to you, how much He loves you, and how He dwells on the inside of you. He has already made your name great. But God remembered Jochebed. Moses was birthed from a woman of worth. Her name was Jochebed, whose name means God's glory. She was a godly woman of remarkable strength, wisdom, courage, ingenuity, and trusted in the promises of God. From early on, she recognized that there was something special about her youngest child. Jochebed did not even need a midwife for this delivery; she gave birth to this promise all by herself. Your purpose is never about you. It is about what you must give birth to. That very thing God placed in you must come forth. Even the basket Jochebed placed Moses in, each layer of the basket was strategically crafted so that nothing would harm Him. Protect your purpose, protect your peace.

To conclude this story, Jochebed went to Pharaoh's palace and nursed Moses until he was seven years old; she was paid while there, and nobody ever knew she was Moses' biological mother. When you know your passion, when you know your purpose, when you know peace, it is there you find your reward. You just show up, be great, and do what you were assigned to do (Exodus 2:1-10 and Exodus 6:20).

Embrace passion, purpose, and peace. Know that you are intoxicating, beautiful, and full of God's glory. You represent the fullness of everything He desires. You represent His peace. He cherishes you, enjoys you, and believes in you. He chose to live within you. He has placed peace inside of you, and now this peace flows from the streams of passion streams from your heart, living waters spring up out of your belly, purpose keeps you alive, virtue covers you, and peace is your reward. Everywhere you go, God's fragrance

of peace drips from your life. You are a rose that intoxicates God's heart, and the fragrance of your rose changes any atmosphere you enter.

So, every God idea, every thought, every creative and innovative design, every business, every non-profit, every book, every song, every concept God has placed inside of you, release it back to God and watch it come to fruition. God gave it to you. He trusted you with it. He saw the finished work before you saw the vision. When you align your passion, purpose, and peace to God's thoughts toward you, He will take the invisible and make it visible, and there is your reward, God's unfailing love and kindness toward you.

Therefore, I leave you with the following questions:

What is your passion?

What is your purpose?

How will you achieve your peace, and what would this look like for you?

I am Dr. Tasheka L. Green. Education is my calling, teaching is my gift, inspiring is my passion, serving is my purpose, and peace is my reward.

Dr. Tasheka L. Green is a transformational servant leader who leads with the heart of a servant but the mind of a leader. Dr. Tasheka L. Green is a wife, mother of three, influential educator, transformational coach, thought-provoking speaker, visionary, fifteen-time bestselling author, philanthropist, and the 2022 Maryland Mother of the Year for American Mothers, Inc.

Dr. Green is the founder and host of two talk shows, "Reflect, Assess, and Adjust" and "Moms, We See You." Dr. Tasheka L. Green leaves her audiences transformed, inspired, energized, and renewed. Her competency in education, servant leadership, and transformational coaching influences personal, professional, leadership, and educational development in the individuals she meets, teaches, and reaches.

Over 20 years of experience as an educator and viewing leadership not as a title or position but as a calling with a greater purpose allowed Dr. Green to birth To Everything There is a Season, Inc. To Everything There is a Season Inc. provides personal, professional, leadership, and educational development to individuals and organizations through a blended coaching and consultation model that supports them in leveraging their talent, passion, and purpose to maximize their greatest potential.

Dr. Green often shares, “Legacy is not what you accomplished, but what you have prepared others to do.” She is carrying out her mother’s life and legacy while building a legacy for others so they, too, can impact and influence the earth.

Website: www.2eseasons.com www.tashekagreen.com www.2eseasonslearn.com

Facebook: drtashekagreen

Instagram: drtashekagreen

LinkedIn: drtashekalgreen

Email: ceo-seasons@outlook.com

Peacefully Pursuing My God-Given Purpose
My Pain but God's plan

DR. ONIKA SHIRLEY

"Peace is a journey of a thousand miles, and it must be taken one step at a time."

~ Lyndon B. Johnson

Life has a way of offering unsolicited surprises. From day to day, you never know what you may have to face, nor do you know the challenges that you may have to overcome. In hindsight after many challenges in my personal life, I can clearly see how it took courage, strategy, and strength. It also took me having my own personal powerful belief system. I thank God I have been able to rise above all the obstacles and embrace the surprises. As a nine-year-old, to hear the words "your grandmother just called and said your daddy passed away" was hard and confusing at the same time being I didn't really understand what that really meant, and then the following year at ten years old having to start working on the journey of overcoming being molested by a public school teacher on a public school field trip that was supposed to be a reward for working hard but rapidly turned into a two-decade nightmare. At the age of 11, I was preparing to run in a race on a Friday morning. I was anxious and excited to only discover as I attempted to get up that I could not bend my left knee. I was taken to a clinic in a small town about 25 minutes away from home and later sent from there to see an orthopedic another 30 minutes away. After being seen it was discovered by the orthopedic that the joint in my left knee never fully grew together which resulted in me being in a straight leg cast from the top of my thigh down to my toes for six weeks. These three moments in my life were all certainly a surprise.

In all three cases, what I was seeing is not what I saw. I knew these were not the plans that God had for me. In Jeremiah 29:11 (MSG) God said "I know what I'm doing. I have it all planned out—plans to take care of you, not abandon you, plans to give the future you hope for." Simply knowing what God had said placed me on a path of perseverance, persistence, and actively seeking his promises.

PURPOSE

There's something about knowing why we are here and what the meaning of our life is. God wants us to find answers to these questions through our walk of faith and as our relationship with him continues to grow and get stronger. Our gifts will reveal our purpose and when we believe every good and perfect gift is from above, we are heading on the path to bringing God great glory. Sometimes we as people will link our careers and business accomplishments with our identity, which can lead to us falling short of our true God-given purpose in life. I believe to live a life with both passion and purpose we must continue to learn who Jesus Christ is and what he says our purpose in life is. We're created in his image so his life reflects many character traits we should seek to live out daily, as we serve God's other children.

Seven steps to discovering your God-given purpose in life

1. Dedicate time to read the word of God
2. Pray and ask God for direction
3. Follow the will of God

4. Live a purpose-driven life
5. Seek first the Kingdom of God
6. Seek solutions to what the world needs
7. Evaluate situations that have hurt you the most and seek the lesson and leave the pain

Personal Process

Good thing, bad thing, who knows?

When things happened to me, I learned not to label them as bad things, and I found that I didn't suffer, but I was able to pick up the broken pieces and start to put things back together.

I asked God to reveal to me my life's purpose. I found that finding a sense of purpose played a vital role in my purpose discovery in the face of difficulties. Life without the guidance of a father was difficult, but I decided to focus my energy on knowing that God had his reasons for me being here and despite the things I went through that it was not because He didn't love me, and neither was it because He didn't care. I found for me to help the world I had to have hands-on experience. God knew what I could handle; he made me, and he made you too. I built positive beliefs in my abilities. It was important for me to have confidence in my abilities. I reminded myself of my strengths, of all the things I was good at doing, and my accomplishments. I did not permit myself to dwell on negative things that I couldn't control. A positive mindset in every situation has helped me build resilience for future challenges, and it helped me overcome some of life's biggest surprises with peace of mind and without bitterness toward God.

I learned to invest in the process, not the outcome. I started to focus on the process of making my vision a reality and not the vision itself. The vision set the direction, but I had to concentrate on the actions necessary to accomplish the vision. I focused on the joy of pursuing my dream, the process, the journey, and not the destination. I learned to envision completed processes. I started to envision the actions I needed to take to ensure the process was completed and that I had done all that I could do to reach my life's goals. So, I didn't focus on the failures, but I focused on finishing.

Resilience is that indescribable quality that allowed me to be knocked down by some of life's toughest situations. However, it has helped me to build inner strength and, in some cases, to come back at least as strong as I was before. Resilience is not magical; it takes real mental work to transcend hardship. Inner strength is about having the courage to face the pain and disappointment without allowing them to crush our spirit.

PEACE

As we go through life, we are hit with many surprises that could lead us to be shaken and left with little faith. During these times the enemy will try to put us in despair and bitterness toward God, but we can't forget all the times God delivered us. We must be on guard because as we are going through them the enemy will try to attack. In our moments of trial and tribulation, we must cry out to God and always remember that we have victory in Christ. While I was going through this, the Lord gave me comfort, encouragement, and motivation, and He was working behind the scenes on my behalf. He reminded me time after time in His word that He will never leave me and that he would never forsake me. James 1:12 says that "God blesses those who patiently endure testing and temptation. Afterward, they will receive the crown of life that God has promised to those who love him." Despite what we go through in life, discovering our God-given purpose will allow us to experience His peace. The apostle Paul said: "Who shall separate us from the love of Christ? shall tribulation, or distress, or persecution, or famine, or nakedness, or peril, or sword?" The world's peace is different from God's peace.

Worldly peace is temporary, short-lived, and dependent upon certain circumstances. God's peace is permanent and eternal, and it's offered through the solution of Jesus and His presence in our lives. The notion of God's peace being able to guard and protect us can be a breath of fresh air for our troubled souls. We don't have to drown in our circumstances and our hearts don't have to be filled with fear and confusion. When circumstances are free of conflict, we enjoy momentary peace, but our God offers peace during life's conflicts, circumstances, and unsolicited surprises. His peace doesn't change with the circumstances; it is secure despite the circumstances. Philippians 4:7: "Then you will experience God's peace, which exceeds anything we can understand. His peace will guard your hearts and minds as you live in Christ Jesus."

God's peace is built on the unshakable and unchangeable foundation of his Word. It's so good to know that God's peace is ours to have because Jesus heals our roots of sin. Reconciliation with God in Christ and the gift of his Holy Spirit allows us the opportunity to enjoy the blessing of peace in our daily lives even when we find ourselves during situations, circumstances, and life's biggest surprises. Are you on the path to experiencing His peace?

Dr. Onika L. Shirley is the Founder and CEO of Action Speaks Volume, Inc. She is a procrastination strategist and behavior change expert and known for building unshakable confidence, stopping procrastination, and getting your dreams out of your head into your life. She is a master storyteller, international speaker, serves in global ministry, an international bestselling author, international award recipient, serial entrepreneur, and global philanthropist impacting lives in the USA, Africa, India, and Pakistan. Dr. O is a motivational speaker and Christian counselor. Dr. Onika is the founder and director of Action Speaks Volume Orphanage Home and Sewing School in Telangana State, India; founder, and director of Action Speaks Volume Sewing School in Khanewal and Shankot, Pakistan. She founded, operated, and visited an orphanage home in Tuni, India for four years and she supported widows in Tuni, India. She is the founder of Empowering Eight Inner Circle, ASV C.A.R.E.S, ASV Next Level Living Program, and P6 Solutions and Consulting. She has served more than 13 years as a therapeutic foster parent for the State of Arkansas while also remaining involved in her local community. Of all the things Dr. O does she is most proud of her profound faith in Christ and her opportunity to serve the body of Christ globally. Dr. O. faithfully walks and serves in many capacities to make a difference in the lives of others. As a human rights and anti-trafficking advocate and consultant she is dedicated to bringing awareness to our 30 human rights and ensuring others are aware that they have human rights and responsibilities.

She spearheaded a book project creating a new author in Nigeria, recipient of I Change Nations Global Leadership Award as an exemplary global leader, and named as A Woman of Excellence "I Change Nations" World Civility.

Facebook: Onika Shirley

Instagram: actionspeaksvolume

Website: actionspeakvolum.com

Email: actionspeaksvolume@gmail.com

My Journey to Inner Peace

DR. THERESA A. MOSELEY

"The life of inner peace, being harmonious and without stress, is the easiest type of existence." —Norman Vincent Peale.

Can you imagine waking up every day and watching the sunrise, hearing the birds chirping, sipping coffee, and watching the news on your phone? That sounds peaceful and serene. Unfortunately, almost every day I wake up, I hear about violence the night before. Most recently I read about a young child 5 months old hit by stray bullets. I read about nine people killed in Baltimore the night before. You never know what to expect when you go out. Many people have their groceries delivered to their homes. They prefer Netflix at home rather than the Friday night at the movie theater. They shop online and stay out of the malls. The fear is real. There are so many young people dying in our country. The violence has peaked over the years and the news coverage of school shootings, mass shootings, road rage, and hate crimes has caused me to speak and write messages on what we all can do, to make the world a more peaceful place.

During this journey, I discovered that by using my gift (voice and intuition), my passion (serving others), and my purpose (to help make the world a peaceful place), I became successful, fulfilled, and have inner peace. Norman Vincent Peale's quote on inner peace is on point. It is the easiest type of existence. The question is, "How do you get there?" "What's the pathway?" In this chapter, I will share my stories about my pathway to inner peace starting with all my trials over the years. You will see through every obstacle or trial; a lesson was learned and therefore I made the negative experience a positive one.

My first recollection as a child was on my third birthday. I had four brothers and we were all lined up on a bench. My dad was in the Army and anytime we were all lined up together, I knew we were getting shots. I cried and screamed because I was scared. This day was different. There was a man with a large device in his hand and he kept flashing a bright light and all this powder was in the air. I did not know what he was doing and that scared me too. Finally, my father came into the room. He saw me crying. He asked me what was wrong. I told him I was afraid. My dad told me the light was a flash, and that we were taking professional pictures. He told me nothing would harm me. I trusted my dad and he stayed until the pictures were done. I still have that picture with my sad eyes and pouting lips. In my mind, I was thinking, "I wish someone would have told me what was going on before we were lined up." Perhaps I would have smiled for the picture. My father was my protector. He knew me better than anyone. We could be miles away and he would call me at the same time I thought about calling him. He used to worry about me traveling so much and moving to places where I knew no one. Then one day he said to me, "I don't have to worry about you anymore. You are doing well. You are so smart and beautiful. You can do anything you want to do." My dad was so proud of me. Unfortunately, he passed away when I was 30. The last day I saw him alive was the day I graduated from college. On that day he was very ill. His lung cancer had him so weak, that he could not attend the ceremony, but he was waiting for me when I returned from the ceremony. I handed him my diploma and he said to me, "I am so proud of you. This diploma is worth a million dollars. Now go live in your purpose." My dad had an eighth-grade education but the wisdom of a sage. I remember him telling me there was no glass ceiling for me. "Knock those suckers down." I was very blessed to have a caring, loving, supportive father. When he passed away 6 months later, I went into a deep state of depression. I would not eat, sleep, bathe, drink or work. I was wasting away. One day as I sit on the floor in my bedroom, a voice from within told me to. “Get up. You are still here. Now go live in your purpose. I am with you.” That shocked me. I looked around and said that was the voice of God or my dad, but whoever it was, it made me realize I have work to do. I got up, bathed, ate, and slowly went back to work. I decided to go back to school to get my Master's Degree in Guidance and Counseling and finally a Doctor of Philosophy Degree. I was very successful working in education. I won major awards including Prince George’s County Chamber of Commerce Outstanding Educator after only 3 years of service. Every degree I received increased my salary and I was able to buy two houses.

One morning in 2011 I woke up and realized my life had changed 360 degrees. I owned two homes and just 30 years ago I was homeless for three days. I rode a city bus all day wondering what to do. I stopped to get off at Leisure World before I realized it was a retirement community. The bus driver looked at me as tears rolled down my cheeks and he knew I was in a crisis. He drove me back to Garden Grove and left me at a mall stop. I prayed to God to help me. My promise was if I could help anyone in a homeless situation in the future I would and I will always have a plan when I do anything else. I will be independent and strong. When I opened my eyes, I saw a church The Crystal Palace Cathedral and I saw a club. I went to the club. I laugh about that now, but in the club, I found my guardian angel who provided a safe place for me to stay for 3 days. I could have stayed longer, but I figured out what I had to do. I re-enlisted in the Army and the rest is history. This time when I got out of the military, I had a plan, a blueprint, a place to stay, and an acceptance into college. The lesson I learned is you must always have a plan of action when you do anything. You must have faith and know that there is a solution to every problem. You must do the work. When I train individuals now, part of the process of discovering their purpose is knowing their gift and passion, doing what they love to do, and developing a blueprint with strategies, and monitoring.

Being homeless was just one of the many trials in my life. As the years passed by while I worked in education, I realized I was successful but not fulfilled. I began to second guess if I was living in my purpose. Some tragic events would lead me to discover that there was more work for me to do. In 2013, one of my students was shot to death. This student was a star athlete. He could have gone to college and played pro ball. Two weeks before he was killed, I had a 15-minute conversation with him during lunch. I asked him what his gift was. He immediately stood up and told me with a big smile, "I play football!" I told him the same effort he puts in learning the playbook and the strength and conditioning, he needs to put into his academics. I told him I would help him graduate from high school, but he must do the work. I sent him to class after our conversation. As he walked down the hall, I began to cry. That was my intuition telling me something was about to happen. Two weeks later he was dead. I was crushed and I had to speak at his funeral. Almost a year later, one of my students was beaten to death in a park. He was a brilliant artist. Both young men's lives mattered. Barack Obama said, "Every life must be given the chance to realize its full potential—that every life matters." My two students' lives were taken before they could live out their divine assignment. Israel was a brilliant surrealist artist. Brandon could have been in his fifth year in the NFL. I started a campaign for No More Violence – One School, One Community, One County at a Time. We wore T-shirts to promote non-violence every Friday. Two years later, I joined a master's class. In the class, the instructor quoted Mark Twain, "There are two days that are important in your life. The day you were born, and the day you find out why." One that day, I realized my gift was my voice and intuition, my passion was serving others, and my purpose was to make the world a peaceful place. I began to speak and write messages on inner peace, world peace, non-violence, and leadership. The pain of losing my students turned into purpose. I wrote my signature bestselling book *Creating Ambassadors of Peace* and spoke around the world on how to become an Ambassador of Peace. When I started helping other people discover their purpose and find inner peace, I became successful, fulfilled, and now I have inner peace. The journey was long, but I'm not finished yet. You can start your journey to inner peace by following the steps below.

Step 1 – Self-discovery. Know your truth. Recognize that you were born with a purpose.

Step 2 – Learn from your trials and tribulations along the way.

Step 3 – Network with others that have the same interest.

Step 4 – Self care. Meditate daily and release any stress.

Step 5 – Love one another and love yourself.

Step 6 – Forgive those who have wronged you.

Step 7 – Serve others. You will find this rewarding.

Step 8 – Eat healthily. Health is wealth.

Step 9 – Use your gift, know your passion, and live in your purpose. This will lead to inner peace.

Remember: Life is but a short road to our ultimate destiny. Make peace, have compassion, and learn to love before you get there.

Dr. Theresa A. Moseley is originally from Fayetteville, North Carolina. She is a United States Army veteran, eight-times bestselling author, three-times international bestselling author, three-times award-winning educator, and an international motivational speaker. During the last year, she received ten awards and recognitions, including Women of Virtue Walking in Excellence. In June 2022, Dr. Moseley was recognized as one of the Top 30 Unstoppable Women Entrepreneurs of 2022.

Dr. Moseley is the owner and chief executive officer of TAM Creating Ambassadors of Peace LLC. Her company provides professional development on transformational leadership and how to create a positive climate in the workplace that promotes inner peace. She uses her bestselling signature book, *Creating Ambassadors of Peace*, to discuss 16 steps to have inner peace. Dr. Moseley has been featured in over 300 news articles, and several magazines including *Tap In*, *Women of Dignity, MySisterKeeper, Vision and Purpose Magazine, The Black Family Magazine, Called to Inspire Magazine, Keynote Magazine,* and *Speakers Magazine*. Dr. Moseley was also recognized as one of the Top 25 Women to Watch in 2022, by *Women of Dignity Magazine*. Dr. Moseley was featured on the cover of *FACE of WOHA Magazine* and was recognized as an empowered woman who works to change the lives of others by helping women find inner peace by living in their purpose. She also will receive the Women of Heart Award, Impacting Peace in the World in London, England on November 12, 2022.

Dr. Moseley retired from the field of education in June of 2022, after 28 years of service. In 1999 she was awarded the Excellence in Education Award from the Prince George's County Chamber of Commerce. In 2006, she was recognized as Prince George's County Outstanding Educator. During her time as an assistant principal at Walker Mill Middle School, she received the Excellence in Gifted and Talented Education Award from the Maryland Department of Education. Dr. Moseley attended Leadership: An Evolving Vision at Harvard Graduate School of Education and the Harvard Institute on Critical Issues in Urban Special Education. She also participated in the Summer Leadership Institute at the Yale Child Study Center – School Development Program. Dr. Theresa currently has 12 books in her bookstore on her website: *The Fourth Child: Five Decades of Hope, Two Decades Apart, Women of Virtue Walking in Excellence, You are Enough, Creating Ambassadors of Peace: 16 Steps to Become an Ambassador of Peace, I AM S.H.E, Step Into Leadership Greatness, Step Into Leadership Greatness Volume 2 Leaders Producing Leaders, What's God Got to Do with It, Eight Qualities of Exceptional Black Women, Unleash Your Undeniable Impact,* and *Passion Purpose Peace – The Pathway through Trials and Tribulations*. Dr. Theresa will add five more books to her collection this year: *The Voice of the Empowered Women, Lioness: Prayers and Affirmations for Women Leaders, Daddy's Girl: Living after the loss of a Legend,* and *Girl, Get Up and WIN Every day: 100 Days of Motivation. Passion Purpose Peace: Pathways through Trials and Tribulations* is her first anthology as a visionary author.

Website: www.creatingambassadorsofpeace.com

Facebook: Dr. Theresa A. Moseley

Instagram: drtheresaamoseley

LinkedIn: Dr. Theresa A. Moseley

Twitter: CreatingTam

YouTube: Dr. Theresa A. Moseley

Email: theresaamoseley2@gmail.com

Speaker Profile:https://speakerhub.com/speaker/dr-theresa-a-moseley

A Journey from Fear to Happiness and Freedom

MARTEKA LANDRUM

"For I know the plans and thoughts that I have for you,' says the Lord, 'plans for peace and well-being and not for disaster, to give you a future and a hope." Jeremiah 29:11 AMP

For most of my life, I have had breathing problems. This was diagnosed as asthma. This came at an early age. I have constantly had people telling me what I can't do. Don't run too much, don't play too hard, don't stay out in the cold, don't eat corn nuts, don't laugh too much, and on and on and on. You see if I did these things, they led to having an asthma attack. It was hard to just be a kid because I was laying somewhere just trying to breathe. When a person has an asthma attack, it's like trying to breathe through a straw. The airways are literally closing. You must take medicine to relax the muscles so air can flow freely to your lungs.

As a result of these breathing problems, I did not participate much in sports. However, I did start walking. In the last few years, I decided to try running. I started slowly because I was not trying to get sick or end up in the hospital. A few years ago, I lived in a large apartment complex and frequently walked there. One day I decided to jog to the dumpster. Once I reached it, I walked to the next one. By the end of my walk, I felt good. I continued this pattern on the next walk. Of course, I had an inhaler in my pocket, but I never needed it. All this time I had been believing these lies that I could not do much exercising. The next thing I know, I'm running around the complex instead of walking. Then I also take my running into the neighborhood. I love the freedom I feel when I run. This experience gave me hope for more. What else can I do that 'they' said I couldn't do? As more lies were uncovered, I learned how to replace them with the truth. The more truth was revealed, the more peace I had. As I learned to become more resilient, my purpose began to get clearer and there was an increase in my inner peace. This inner peace felt like warm sunshine on a beach. I could hear the waves coming in and going out. I felt the warm sand between my toes, the sun on my back, and a gentle breeze as my inner peace increased.

Not having the freedom to play was painful. My purpose is to help others get free. I was in my twenties when I began to realize that my gift was my voice and ability to reach others with my insight. Not long after that, my passion began to take shape: helping others find their truth.

Here are the steps I took to turn my pain into purpose: self-discovery, discovering my gift, setting short and long-term goals to follow through on my passion, reflecting on where I am, and sharing my wisdom with the world. I spent a long time in the self-discovery stage and reflecting. I had to get my mind right about the lies I was believing and some fears I had.

Lies are intended to keep us out of or hinder our relationships with others. Dictionary.com defines a lie as: "a false statement made with deliberate intent to deceive; an intentional untruth." For years I was believing lies: no one will listen, you are too young, no one will believe you, and it doesn't matter. Not only did these lies come in, but fear did as well. These lies were shouted over and over so much that I began to believe them. This combination of believing these lies and operating out of fear caused many problems. I was not fulfilling my destiny because my belief system was wrong, and I had lots of fears. There were so many things connected with these lies and fears. I soon realized this caused a breakdown in relationships from seeds of doubt that were planted along with those lies. Over 30 years of my life had been marked by insecurities, lack of trust, affirmation, and validation, anxiety, sorrow, false comfort, brokenness, fear of rejection, no sense of identity, and no voice of love and blessing.

Then began the time when I would be healed of all these fears. As healing was taking place, I'd discover something new about myself or my gift. I reflected by journaling. This went on for many years. Self-discovery helps you become aware of who you are. Your authentic self. Have you met them? Do you really know who you are? What do you like to do? What do you not like? What are your goals? You are not who 'they' thought you were. Who are you? Self-discovery is a beautiful thing. You will need to try new things to see if you like them. This is how you learn to accept freedom.

Along the way, you will discover your gift. Everyone was born with a unique footprint. Your gift is already in you. Tap into that gift. It's important that you can tell others what your gift is. T. D. Jakes said, "If you can't figure out your purpose, figure out your passion. For your passion will lead right into your purpose." Discover what your gift is and set goals.

Set short- and long-term goals to follow through on your passion. Have you ever heard of SMART goals? They are specific, measurable, attainable, realistic, time-oriented goals connected to your passion. You want to be sure to monitor them every week.

You also want to reflect on where you are. What have you learned in the last six months? What are some positive things you're doing that are helping you move forward in your passion that you weren't doing six months ago? When we reflect on where we are it helps us to not be overwhelmed. So, make a list of what you are doing now that is moving you towards your goals. Make a list of the things that you've done in the last 6 months that are helping you live out your passion.

Lastly, you want to share your wisdom with the world. When you are happy, you can spread sunshine to everybody else. There are things you learned along the way that have been very beneficial for you and it might help someone else. Be willing to share your story. Share your experiences with others so they can glean from your wisdom, can move forward in their goals, and achieve their passion by you sharing your wisdom. We've all been through stuff. You get to decide what you want to do with it. Writing and speaking are how I share my wisdom and experiences.

I have been blessed to have many people help me on this journey: youth leaders, family, friends, counselors, and community members. The one that stands out is a counselor who gave me a notebook and said to write. As I started living in my purpose, all the questions I had about my purpose began to fade away. I'm no longer wondering what I'm supposed to do.

What a difference healing makes. Freedom to me is being like a child again. You have no worries. You are free to express yourself in any way: laughing, jumping, dancing. Being free is knowing who you are and being okay with it. Being free is believing in yourself. Freedom is such a wonderful feeling. When you have lived in fear for so long and it's finally all gone, you feel lighter. The grass is greener. The sky is bluer. The sun shines brighter. You begin to feel happiness on a level that you've never felt before. Maybe you've never been happy. It's a good feeling. It's a wonderful feeling. Freedom exposes the lies, replaces them with truth, and realizes it's okay to be different. Freedom helps you get out of the box that you or others put yourself into. Bad things happen in life, but you get to choose if you're going to let your emotions be in control or not.

Thucydides said, "The secret to happiness is freedom. The secret to freedom is courage." Are you courageous enough to take off the mask to show who you really are? Who is your authentic self? Have you been courageous enough to discover your gift? It's already inside of you. What are you passionate about? Have you set short- and long-term goals to courageously follow your passion? Are you reflecting on where you are and courageously sharing your wisdom with the world? If the secret to happiness is freedom, and if the secret to freedom is courage, then my friend, you must take a step forward. Step up, step out, or continue your journey. Phone a friend, get a coach, go to therapy, go for a walk, just don't step back. Your journey from sadness and fear to happiness and freedom takes forward movement. You have great strength. You are courageous. You are an overcomer.

Marteka Landrum is a coach for challenging teens. She works with schools and parents by meeting teens where they are to help them understand how their actions are impacting others, get clear on who they are, and give them coping and communication strategies so that they can finally feel understood, have success in school, and have better relationships so everyone can find peace. Marteka received a Bachelor of Arts in Education from Wichita State University with certification in English as a Second Language. She loves to cook, sing, travel, and help others find their truth. Marteka published her first book, *Broken Warrior: Be Empowered to Overcome*, in 2021.

Website: www.positivechanges11.com.

Facebook: Marteka Landrum

Instagram: positive_changes11

Living on Purpose

NADIA MONSANO

"Peace of mind is the direct result of self-satisfaction in knowing you did your best to become the best version of yourself."

As my mother drove off in the taxi that was taking her to the airport to travel to America, I felt so sad to know that I was not going to see her for a while. I was 13 years old at the time when my mother made the tough decision to leave me with my grandmother. She wanted to start building a better foundation for me and our family to have a better life. That day was a sad day for me to see my mom leaving and not knowing when I would be able to see her again. As the taxi got further away where I could no longer see it, I ran straight to my grandmother's arms and cried. In a gentle voice my grandmother said to me, "My darling granddaughter, everything is going to be fine." She continued, "In God's timing we will see her again and the next time we see her we will celebrate her accomplishments." My mother called every weekend to check in on us and every month she would send barrels of supplies that we would need for the home and surprises for me.

Two years later I got the call I was waiting for. With excitement in my mother's voice over the phone, she said, "It is time for you and your grandmother to come live with me." She paused for a moment to hear my reaction. All I could remember doing was uncontrollably crying because I was overjoyed. Once I pulled myself together, I started to ask a million questions, as a teenager would. The most important question was, "When can I come and live with you forever Mom?" She laughed and said, "Next month the same taxi that came and took me to the airport is going to come and get you and your grandmother so you all can take a flight." I replied, "I am going to be anxiously waiting." I gave the phone to my grandmother so my mother could go over the details with her. I immediately ran across the street to my friend's house to share the great news. She was so happy for me. We would miss each other but she knows how much I wanted to be back with my mother.

The day finally arrived; it was time to head to the airport. I was packed and sitting outside anxiously waiting for the taxi to arrive. As the taxi drove off with my grandmother and me, we waved goodbye to our neighbors. I was filled with all types of emotions. I was sad because I did not know when I would see my friends again, I was excited to get to the airport, and nervous because I had never taken a flight before, and I did not know what to expect. As I looked through the back window of the taxi all I could see was the neighborhood that I grew up in disappearing. I got comfort in knowing that it was time to close this chapter of building childhood memories with my friends and open a new chapter for my life in America with my mother. The three-hour flight felt like forever, but it was worth it.

After settling down with my mom it was time to get registered for high school. On the first day of school, I walked into this huge building. I felt so overwhelmed as I walked to the counselor's office. I did a brief introduction, and the counselor gave me a tour and dropped me off to my first class. The class was filled with so many white Americans, which was a culture shock to me. You see in my neighborhood back in Trinidad we all spoke alike, and we were all similar in complexion. The teacher showed me where my assigned seat was. After settling in the class, we had an assignment that we had to turn in. After the teacher was finished grading the assignment she came to the front of the classroom and started to hand out our papers. Sitting in front of me was Jennifer. When the teacher handed Jennifer my paper to pass back to me, she threw my paper on the floor and uttered the words, "Fetch your paper from the floor Black slave." I was so embarrassed and shocked to hear the names she called me. The teacher immediately sent her to the principal's office, and she got suspended for a day. Jennifer lived in my neighborhood and that evening after school we ended up getting on the same school bus. She was so mad that she got suspended that she started to tell her friends about what happened. I am such a quiet person, and I did not know anyone on the bus. I sat by myself. In the back of the bus, I could hear their conversation about me. They degraded me for the color of my skin and the way I spoke with an accent. I tried my best to hold back the tears, but I couldn't. It was the first time in my life that I wished I could change the color of my skin in order to fit in and not be called names because I looked and spoke differently. On several occasions the bus driver would tell the group to stop calling me names. They saw that I was in tears and realized that I was new on the bus. When the bus stopped in my neighborhood, I quickly got off the bus and ran home. When I got to my front door, I was breathing heavy and uncontrollably crying. I tried to wipe the tears from my face before I entered the house.

When I entered my home, my grandmother was sitting in the living room waiting for me to come home to tell her how my first day of school was. When she saw me come through the door, she was shocked to see my face. In a hysterical voice, she asked, "Nadia what is wrong, why are you crying?" I ran straight to her arms and with my voice trembling I said, "I hate the color of my skin, I will never fit in here in America." My grandmother went and got me a glass of water to calm me down. She hugged me until I stopped crying and gently rubbed my back to console me. Once I got my composure, she put her hands in mine and made me look directly into her eyes. In a gentle voice, she said to me, "My darling granddaughter, you were born in the image and likeness of God, and he made no mistake when he created you." As she wiped the tears that were falling from my eyes she continued, "Your Black is beautiful, and no one can take that from you." She explained to me that I was in a place of diverse cultures and sometimes when someone does not understand another person's culture, they make fun of it. My grandmother reminded me that my uniqueness is what sets me apart from everyone and I should never try to fit in anywhere. I should stand out from the crowd and embrace my uniqueness. I told my grandmother about what happened to me in school. She was so upset but she stayed calm enough to let me know that what happened to me is not something that is tolerated, and she was happy to know that the student got suspended. She made sure I knew that no one should see me sweat under pressure and never waste tears on someone who does not deserve it. My grandmother always had a way with words that would comfort me and this time her words also made me realize that my Black is beautiful, and my accent is a part of my culture. I should never want to change anything about myself to fit in.

The next day when I went back to school my teacher had me stand in front of the classroom and let all the students know that we all must respect each other, and we should embrace other cultures. She made me introduce myself and describe where I came from and at the end of my story I said, "Therefore my Black skin is beautiful, and my accent makes me unique." The students were so fascinated by my culture that they started to do research on the traditions and foods. After that day I made some close friends and they accepted me for who I am and not what I looked and sounded like. From that day forward I walked around the school with my head held high knowing that God did not make a mistake in creating me. I will always embrace my culture. Even though my grandmother is no longer here with me in my adult life, I am forever grateful to her for teaching me to love myself and never try to change to fit in anywhere. I am at peace with myself knowing that My Black Is Beautiful.

Nadia Monsano is an international bestselling author, marketing and branding specialist, and a retired veteran staff sergeant after serving 10 years in the US Army. While in the military Nadia served one tour in Iraq and earned the Iraqi Freedom Medal of Honor. After retiring from the Army Nadia started working in corporate America in the medical field as a program director.

Nadia started her own company My Sister Keeper in February 2020. My Sister Keeper is a branding and marketing agency that offers graphic designs. Nadia has worked with women all over the United States and internationally to help them launch their businesses and show up in the digital market professionally.

Nadia has her own positive quotes apparel brand called MSK Apparel, which she uses to spread positivity through apparel throughout the world. Nadia is the co-founder of a non-profit organization Step Toward Awareness. Step Toward Awareness is a community development, project-based non-profit organization. Working together with individuals, non-profit organizations, and businesses, the organization produces unique programs, fundraising events, and solutions to maximize the value of supporters and the community they serve. In May of 2020 Step Toward Awareness hosted Lyrics of Love concert virtually and raised thousands of dollars for our front-line workers in the most challenging times that our nation was facing. This event provided 200 care packages for front-line workers.

Nadia launched the *My Sister Keeper Magazine* in October of 2020. This magazine is used as a give-back program to the community. Nadia also uses this magazine line to provide opportunities for entrepreneurs and business owners to obtain visibility, credibility & profitability for their products and service through promotion in the *MSK Magazine*. Since October Nadia has donated thousands of dollars to St. Jude Children's Hospital, The Downs Syndrome Foundation, The Lupus Foundation, and The Timalechi nursery school of Embangweni, Malawi. *MSK Magazine* will continue to make an impact one issue at a time.

Website: www.mysisterkeeper.biz

Facebook: mysisterkeeperforever

Instagram: mysisterkeeper

YouTube: mysisterkeeperforever

A Pathway to Discover Your Purpose, Ignite Your Passions and Deliver Ultimate Peace

ANTONIO D. LOVE, COLONEL (RET.) US AIR FORCE, MHA, FACHE

"I will guide you along the best pathway for your life. I will advise you and watch over you." Psalm 32:8

What's your story? In my home, displayed above the entryway of the kitchen and visible from the dinner table where my family and I do life is a sign that reads, "HOME, Where Your Story Begins." For those that I've had the privilege and honor to serve alongside and lead, you know that one of the first questions I ask as we're getting acquainted, is "What is your story?" I ask this simple question because I am a relational being and leader and I believe that life and relationship occur at the intersections of our stories. So, with that in mind, please allow me to share with you my story. Consistent with my life and leadership philosophy to live and lead with L.O.V.E. (Lift with Love and Laughter, Live with Openness That Leads to Unity, Lead with Vision That's Rooted in Values, Excellence Is My Attitude), this story will be filled with lots of LOVE and some laughter, it will be told with OPENESS and TRANSPARENCY, the source of my VISION and origins of my VALUES will be evident and at the conclusion, you can be the judge on whether it was delivered with an attitude of EXCELLENCE.

My story begins in 1952 in rural east central Alabama. That was the year my father, Charlie L. Love, was born. He was the third of my grandmother's 12 children. The family were sharecroppers and would frequently move from farm to farm working the land. Sometimes the moves were by choice, oftentimes they were not. Growing up, the children were expected to work, going to school was secondary to doing your part to support the family. This reality shaped my father's work ethic at a very young age, but also set the foundation for how he would pursue life to this very day. Despite his circumstances, my father graduated from high school and in 1972, joined the United States Air Force. Inspired by his childhood, one of the first things my father purchased was an acre of land where he had a home built for his mother. The principles of hard work and ownership, in every sense of the word, are central to who my father is and are lessons that he not only lives by, but also passed on to my siblings and me. My father is my hero. I stand because he stood and would not be moved. My love and respect for him is immense and I thank him for being a great example of what a man, husband, father, and citizen should be.

My mother, Cassandra F. Love, was born in 1958. She is the oldest and only daughter of my grandmother's four children. My mother was a quiet, studious child who excelled academically. She began her educational journey attending a segregated school. In 1967, when she was only nine years old, my grandmother and her two sisters made the decision that my mother and her cousins would be some of the first to integrate the schools in the community. As an aside, my mother and I share the same high school alma mater. The school that she integrated is the same school I graduated valedictorian some 25 years later. Despite the challenges of her day, my mother continued excellence in the classroom, earning honor roll status, but towards the end of her high school tenure, she encountered a challenge of a different sort, namely…me!!! Yes, my mother was a teenage mother, but she was and is so much more. You see, when my parents found out that I was on the way, my father, doing the honorable thing, proposed marriage to my mother. My mother declined. Wise beyond her years, she said to my father, "I want you to marry me because you want to marry me, not because I'm carrying your child." My father, already in the Air Force, had orders and soon moved to the Philippines. Six months later, my mother received a second proposal via mail along with a ring inside. This time she accepted, and my parents were wed on my mother's birthday, June 22, 1975. I was days short of 15 months old. They have now been married for over 47 years. Besides her family, my mother's other passion is the profession of nursing. For 35 years, the last 33 spent serving our nation's veterans at the VA hospital in Tuskegee, AL, she dedicated her life's work to serving patients all along the spectrum of life. My mother is my inspiration. She gave me life and nurtured in me a sense of compassion, humility, and service and for that I am eternally grateful and blessed to be her son.

In 1977, I gained a brother, Andrus D. Love, and in 1984, I gained a sister Adrienne D. Love. As the oldest sibling, my parents expected that I not only watch out for my brother and sister but more importantly provide a positive example for them to follow. In short, they gave me purpose. I absolutely love being their big brother. My brother Andrus employed his talents and passion as a counselor and grew to be an amazing husband, father, community leader, and advocate. As the baby of the family, Adrienne certainly embodied some of the traditional characteristics of being the baby, but the thing I most admire about her is her passion, compassion, and advocacy for children. It did not surprise me at all to see her become an amazing and inspirational teacher and mother.

As you can probably tell, family is central to my life's story and as I shift to the members of my home, let me just say…my quiver is full! As a former military member, I served, but my family served right alongside me. There are some significant differences though. One of the biggest is when we had to move, I moved right into a job, most of the time, I knew or had knowledge of or had worked with some of the people in the new place, so it was oftentimes an easier transition for me. For my family, it was almost all new every time and that was at times very challenging. Tre, Jaide, Aliyah, Amaris, Shawn, Gracclyn, no matter what title is put in front of my name or letters after, there is no title more important to me than Daddy. My children are my purpose.

Now to my bride, Melissa, but first I need to set the stage. The year was 2012. The place was Frederick, Maryland. The date was June 2. The event, Convoy of Hope, Frederick. Convoy of Hope is a faith-based organization with a mission to serve the underprivileged amongst us. It was an especially long, cold, and snowy winter. In fact, we never really had much of a spring at all that year. When I look back at that season of my life, I'd say the winter season of 2011-2012, and the corresponding weather closely reflected my mood and outlook on life at the time. I had gone through a divorce, was a single dad, and just felt a sense of gloom and heaviness. June 2 was a Saturday. We had intense thunderstorms the night before. The heavy rains drenched the area with so much rain that it threatened the event. Thankfully as dawn broke, the clouds passed and left beautiful blue skies, but it was still on the chilly side. That morning, Aliyah, Amaris, and I headed to the fairgrounds to serve. We reported to the grocery section and began to fill bags with various items and provided them to people and then the call came…they needed to relocate about 20 pallets of potatoes. Hearing the call, I moved to the first pallet, organized a human conveyor system, and began to offload the potatoes. About five bags into the first pallet, I looked up, and there she was. At that moment, my stomach fluttered and before I knew it, my mouth opened and I called, "Excuse me, are you looking for something to do?" Thankfully, she said yes, came over, positioned herself next to me, and labored alongside me for the rest of the morning. We were married 6 months later, and she's been by my side ever since. Melissa was and is my silver lining. My wife ignites my passions. As I recall all the pain and trials in my life, I realized one day I have inner peace now, and leaving a legacy for my family is the purpose of everything I do.

In closing, LIFE happens when you're LIVING. An examination of one's story is a powerful way to discover purpose, ignite passions and deliver ultimate peace. The late, great Muhammad Ali once said, "Service to others is the rent you pay for your room here on earth." Over the course of my life, I've proudly worn the cloth of my country. In that time, my faith in the Most-High God has sustained me, my family has given me a sense of purpose, my freedom has inspired me to service, and the fellowship that I've enjoyed along the way has nourished and replenished my soul. So, my friends, what's your story? Learn from your trials and tribulations, find your gift and passion and live in YOUR purpose. It will lead to inner peace.

Antonio D. Love, Colonel (Ret.) US Air Force, MHA, FACHE is a board-certified healthcare executive with extensive leadership experience within challenging, diverse, and complex healthcare and supply chain environments. His experience spans across inpatient and outpatient service lines, graduate medical education, international markets, integrated health systems, ambulatory surgery, and value-based care. He hails from Tallassee Alabama and received a Bachelor of Science from Samford University and a Master of Healthcare Administration from the University of Alabama Birmingham. He commissioned as a first lieutenant in the United States Air Force Medical Service Corps in 2000 and retired as a colonel in 2021. His illustrious military career included tours in multiple functional disciplines, and three deployments and culminated with three consecutive command tours at the squadron and group levels. Mr. Love is married to the former Melissa Jones, and they are the proud parents of six children Tre', Jaide', Aliyah, Amaris, Shawn, and Gracelyn.

Facebook: Antonio Love

Instagram: Antonio.love.3158

You're Not Listening

JAYLEEN ORTIZ

"Self-awareness is the skeleton key to peace."—Jayleen Ortiz

I am the first-born daughter in what used to be a nuclear Puerto Rican family. I have one younger brother who is truly my first best friend. We were raised sheltered, and only had each other left to create the world we wished we were a part of sometimes. We put on puppet shows, and breaking news segments, and dressed up in any costume imaginable. That's just a very short list of the number of things we came up with to entertain ourselves. I remember my childhood being whimsical, light, and full of laughs. My brother was my partner in crime and when my cousins came over, it was always a good time. We took family trips often and had sit-down dinners almost every night.

My friends, my brother, and my cousins were usually the only constant companions in my life. We argued and fought as any family does, but we were usually solid as a unit. Growing up, I was called the "family lawyer." Any time I would hear my brother or cousins being scolded, I immediately had to defend them. I would notice that their side of the story was not being heard. I did this often enough to annoy the adults and earn the name. I used to be offended by the title because I felt I was only doing what was right, standing up for the people I cared about. In my current enlightenment, I realized that I was doing what I wished people would do for me.

As I said before, my childhood was magical. My parents did their best to keep my brother and me happy, as we never wanted for anything. But during those years, I also got quieter and quieter. Let me explain. I was always a goofy, happy, and energetic child and teenager. Oftentimes that called for people to tell me to "calm down" or "stop being weird." As time went on, I received fewer responses if I got a response at all. I started to say, "Did you hear me?" Then there were the times when I would start a story and would be cut off because someone else started their story instead. I started to feel invisible. I usually only felt seen when I was around my closest friends, the majority of whom I made before the sixth grade. My mother wanted us to have the world and gave it to us, but she also had extremely high expectations of us in order to earn a lot of it. If my handwriting wasn't up to standards, I had to start my homework over. If I brought home a B, the response was always, "What happened to the A?" She was doing her best to ensure that I paid attention to detail and took pride in what I was turning in to my teachers. However, now, I tend to have unrealistic expectations of myself based on everything that was expected of me growing up. If something wasn't perfect, I had the tendency to internalize and tell myself that I wasn't good enough or capable of anything extraordinary.

These experiences ultimately affected my ability to self-advocate and plan my own future. All I knew was home and school for such a long time. When it was time to graduate high school, I was, as they say, "lost in the sauce." I was an honors student with A's and I stayed pretty quiet in classes. I did not feel seen by teachers, or my family and I didn't possess the social skills to express what I was going through. Nor did I truly understand it myself enough to say much. While others applied to universities, I just lived every day to not be yelled at by my parents. I went to college because everyone said I had to and ended up having a few unpleasant experiences my first year on campus. In four years, I switched my major three times, as I still was unsure what I wanted to do for the rest of my life. I studied Criminal Justice and Psychology, and ultimately received an associate degree in Business Administration. The concept of just doing one thing, forever, never sat well with me. I had so many interests and still couldn't settle on one career. I didn't know it then, but I was still operating on the expectations of others.

When I was 24, I was finally ready to move out of my parent's home to be able to dictate my life as I saw fit. I was terrified of the move as I barely had anything saved and I didn't want to let my best friend and roommate down. I made it through, and it was so much fun to finally be responsible for just myself. Very shortly after that, my father packed up and left for Vegas to be with his mistress and I had to step in and take care of what he left behind. My mother was extremely ill at the time, and I felt helpless as I had been thrust into the role of "head of household" and I didn't even live with them anymore. I didn't live alone for long. My father left my mother to pay an extremely high rent bill and knew that this wasn't possible. After seven months after moving out my brother moved into my two-bedroom apartment, and my mother into her sister's extra room. This is where our problems as a family began. I pretended that his abrupt departure didn't affect me for years. However, thanks to him, I was suddenly stressed for money in order to help my family out of the situation they were in.

In 2016, I accepted a job at a bank as I felt it was a practical and sustainable "adult" job and it paid more than I was earning at the makeup counter. For two years though, I was stressed and miserable. I started to lose extreme amounts of weight causing my family and me to worry. My hair was falling out, I was moody, and I suffered through what I called an "existential crisis." I began to question everything I had done in the past and blamed myself for ending up where I was. I felt like I was on autopilot and often felt I wasn't present in my own life. I started to draw and paint again to get in touch with who I used to be before I had to take on so many responsibilities. It did work for a little while, but the noise in my head eventually got too loud. My boyfriend at the time was a huge support system and encouraged me to meditate and ground myself in order to find the peace I sought. Hearts were eventually broken and we're not together today, but I still thank him for those lessons often. His way of encouraging me made me see myself the way I used to when I was a child; whimsical, light, and full of laughs. I realized through meditation that my purpose was greater than what was right in front of me. My passion is to help and encourage people, especially those that couldn't speak up for themselves. I eventually left that miserable job and started to work for the same school system I grew up in. This was my doorway into helping little lost souls find themselves. Although it was a significant pay cut, I was happy to wake up and go to work every day.

I started in the office at an elementary school and then moved up to an in-school suspension monitor at a middle school. At the time, it felt like the perfect fit, and I loved working with that age group. I was in a position where I was applying my entire skill set from college. Criminal justice was applied in the way that in-school suspension is a response to violations of the "school law," or the code of conduct. I used psychology in order to understand the students' motives for their behavior and how I could help. The business aspect came in as I realized that I needed to find ways to reach more people. My objective became to help others understand my approach to discipline and how it breeds results. I was not being heard at the middle school, and eventually, I was tuned out completely. Something I had grown accustomed to, but I refused to accept it this time. I now know I need to follow my dreams my own way and align with people who share my same vision. Instead of yelling at the top of my lungs at the people who aren't listening, I will just speak to the ones that will.

I recently removed myself from that environment and have entered a space where I am not only utilized for all of my skills, but they are also appreciated. The move has aligned me with people who actively listen and share common interests. I was inspired to go back to school and pursue my bachelor's in early childhood education and then my master's in art therapy. I realized that I could combine everything I loved to do into a career that fits me as a person. I no longer will compromise my morals and beliefs to satisfy the expectations people have of me. My purpose is to help people and somehow, I've always known it. Once I started to become more self-aware, I homed in on the skills that brought me the most joy. Living in my purpose has given me my inner peace. I am excited to give back to my community and make a difference. The peace made me stop doubting myself and pushed me into the pursuit of my passion.

Inner peace is having a heightened sense of self and knowing what elements will ground you and bring you balance. I learned how to understand myself in a way that was not taught to me by my parents, teachers, or friends. Through meditation, I was able to unlock the unconscious parts of my mind and understand the root of my trauma. Once I healed that pain, I started to seek peace. In order to get rid of my persona, I began to look inward and discover my strengths and limitations. For years, I strived to be the best version of myself that everyone else thought I should be. When I realized that there was no way to please everyone, I began to do things that brought me peace. Once I started to accept and live in my truth, my life turned around. I challenged myself to be the person I want to be for 30 days. The challenge was to eat, breathe, and sleep as my situational best self. With this perception and approach to life, I have been able to manifest everything that is for me.

My story is still being written; however, I have found peace in pursuit of my passion. I've always been told that I possess the kind of energy that draws others to me, and I didn't know how to use that power until now. I hope my story will inspire others to draw on their own innate energy to heal themselves, have tranquility of the mind, and make their world a better place on their own terms. My core belief is that any one person is capable of infinite paths, it is up to them to choose which one they take. I used to seek happiness, now all I seek is peace.

Jayleen Ortiz is 31 years old and was born and raised in Prince George's County, MD. Growing up, she always had a zest for life and a passion to help others. Her endless curiosity and quick learning ability sharpened a skill set that prepared her to adapt to any situation she faced with. As a child, and now, Jayleen possessed many interests and therefore participated in a variety of activities. However, art and creativity have been a constant for her; so much so that she applies them to how she lives her life today. Jayleen wants to live in a world where mutual understanding and respect is a natural behavior. In order to start making a difference, she started by working in the very school system that made her who she is today. Jayleen believes that by positively impacting the youth of today, there is a chance to better society.

Facebook: Jayleen Ortiz

Instagram: makeupbyjayleen

Transformation to Triumph: Won't He Do It!

Dr. Joi L. Brown

"Greatness is not measured by what a man or woman accomplishes, but by the opposition he or she has overcome to reach the goals."

-Dorothy Height

Change is inevitable. It's going to happen during our lives. Change is hard for many people and even within organizations. Change brings uneasy feelings of not knowing the outcome. We have all heard this before, "We have always done it this way, or why do we need to change it if it is working for us?"

Feelings of uncertainty, fear, anxiety and even frustration make an appearance through our words, actions, and behaviors. Oh, but keep living long enough and you will understand the power of change can also bring growth, interest, hope, and joy. Change is necessary for life and essential to unlocking one's passion and purpose. Change is transformation. In my transformations, I have had to alter, modify, amend, remodel, reshape, redo, reconstruct, rebuild, reorder, revamp, rework, and remake myself to become the best version of myself and step into my greatness. Transformation is part of life's journey.

I know what it feels like to go through multiple transformations at the same time. I have personally dealt with my fair share of life's curve balls and felt like I wanted to give up and throw in the towel at times. Trying to move forward in life but bound by baggage from my past or feeling like I am not good enough. Being overlooked professionally, just to name a few. It was during these moments in my life that my transformation occurred to lead to my triumph.

Change is difficult and it takes time. What happens when you are in an organization that has announced it's going through a transformation? What does that mean? Will I be affected? What about my team? I had question after question with no answers. The change was coming.

Let me rewind the story so you can understand the transformation that is about to manifest. I started my Federal Government career in 2008 as a student intern. It was during the internship that I was exposed to recruiting and hiring. I worked on projects that promoted careers within the Federal Government. My passion to educate and equip people on federal career opportunities was birthed as a student intern. During the internship, I seized every opportunity to meet and learn from others, and I volunteered for projects that allowed me to learn various facets of human resources such as training and development, career development, recruitment, and outreach. After my first summer, I was asked if I wanted to continue to work while earning my degree. I jumped on that opportunity.

I have grown up in the human resource profession and held numerous positions from intern to specialist, to team leader, to supervisor, to now HR director. Won't He do it! Every position I had prepared me for the next one. I was blessed to have mentors who believed in me and were instrumental in my growth and development. My mentors provided me with career and professional advice and introduced me to key people that I was able to work with on projects that allowed me to use various gifts and talents. I was advancing in my career and landed my first supervisor job at the age of 30. Your girl was giving God all the praise. I had a great team and was blessed to have an awesome boss. I witness daily what true leadership was. My boss became my mentor and coach. Life was great until the transformation came.

In a leadership meeting, the transformation was announced, and we had to review the organization and position structure and identify reductions in personnel and operational cost. The bottom line was employees would be downgraded and impacted financially. As part of the transformation team, reviewing the impacted employee list and issuing the formal notification letters was part of my job as human capital branch chief.

One day my boss called me into her office, and I thought nothing of it until she told me I was impacted by the transformation. I was having an out-of-body experience. As she talked to me, I was thinking, "I applied for this position less than a year ago and now you tell me that I am going to be downgraded? Why is this happing to me? What am I going to do? What will my staff and others think?" I left her office, went back into my office, and broke down. I wanted to run out of the building and keep going, but I could not. I prayed and asked the Lord to help me show up during this transformation. This change was too much even for me to handle.

After much prayer, I spoke with my mom, who helped me to remember who I am and that in life our tests can become our testimony. From the day my boss told me I was impacted, I transformed my mindset and told myself this is not a reflection of my talents, gifts, and expertise. I held my head up high and I was going to show up every day and be the Joi that I know I had been called to be. I had to alter and modify my thinking and not stay in my pity party. When unexcepted things happen in life and it's not our fault, it can cause us to stay stuck in a negative space and miss the lesson or growth opportunity.

Showing up each day was not easy, and I truly had to mute other people's opinions and thoughts of me. I could not be consumed by what they were saying or thinking about me. People will always have something to say about you, that's a fact. I learned the power of mute. I muted the negativity from myself and others, and I spoke life into my situation. I had faith to believe I was going to get a new position and I also spoke it out loud. Words have power.

While going through the transformation, I was motivated to rework and revamp my plan. For me to change my situation, I had to do something, I had to act. It was time to move. I had the opportunity to go on a temporary assignment in another organization. I spent two years serving as the Program Manager for a cybersecurity internship program and was instrumental in exposing over 300 student interns in 40 states to cyber work. The program framework that I developed was used to build future cyber programs with congressional funding.

I don't want you to miss how the transformation turned into my triumph. Remember, I had two years before my downgrade was going to be effective. I spent two years on a temporary assignment working on the cybersecurity student internship program. I started my career within the Federal Government as an intern. God's timing is always divine. I was offered a full-time position as supervisor human resource specialist making more money than I made two years before when I first accepted the position. What I thought I would be losing, I was not, and I was going to be making more financially. God gave me triple for my trouble. Won't He do it.

The tips below were all strategies that allowed me to come through my test and share my mighty testimony of transformation to triumph! Won't He do it!

- Transformation to Triumph Tip: Made-up Mindset

Have a committed mindset to know thy self and the gifts, talents, and strengths that you bring to this world. Remind yourself of who you are and the value you bring to others. Your life has purpose and meaning. You must believe in yourself at all costs regardless of others. Remind yourself of who you are. Ambitious, bold, confident, determined, fearless, go-getter, intelligent, etc. You are destined for greatness.

- Transformation to Triumph Tip: Mute the Noise

Mute is a powerful thing. Learn to put the noise from self or others on mute or silence. Use life's remote control and mute negative opinions or perspectives of others, social media, past mistakes, failures, and people saying what you will not do or accomplish. Watch what you let into your mindset. Be bold enough to use the mute in life.

- Transformation to Triumph Tip: Motivated to Move

Motivation is the driving factor for actions and behaviors that causes us to do something. Action or movement is required in life to push through the setbacks, failures, past mistakes, or people not seeing your value or worth. To accomplish a goal, task, or change a situation, action is required. People who reach their greatness in life learn how to move, forge ahead, and take a step toward possibilities.

Change is inevitable. It's going to happen during our lives. In my transformation to triumph, I had a made-up mindset, muted the noise, and was motivated to move. My trials and tribulations have led me to my purpose and now I have inner peace. All I can say is, Won't He Do It!

Dr. Joi L. Brown is a living testament that the "potential for greatness lives within each of us." Being raised on the "I Can" mantra transformed her life to always believe in herself and to walk boldly in her gifts and talents. Joi has motivated thousands to step into their greatness and live a life of purpose. Joi is a career strategist, certified life coach, international bestselling author, empowerment speaker, and entrepreneur known as the "positive energizer." She continues to fulfill her life's motto *"If I can help somebody along this journey called life with a word or song, then my living will not be in vain*" through her professional and community endeavors.

Joi is the chief executive officer of 3EEE Consulting, where she educates, equips, and empowers people through coaching, conversations, and workshops in career and entrepreneur development, conflict resolution, goal setting, health and wellness, leadership, and team development, and personal and professional branding. She has over 24 years of demonstrated human resource development and management expertise in developing and executing human capital programs that achieved organizational goals and objectives. Joi is living her dreams as HR director within the Federal Government.

Joi shares empowering messages as an author of two anthologies, *Step Into Leadership Greatness: Leadership Is Not A Title* and *Silhouettes of Strategies From Authentic Coaches For Mind, Body, and Soul.* She uses her expertise and personal experiences to share with readers how to lead from conflict to collaboration and transform their bodies and mind. As an executive contributor for *Brainz Magazine*, she provides strategies globally on how to be prepared and positioned for life's next opportunity. Joi was recognized as one of

As an empowerment speaker, Joi motivates audiences with her powerful messages to Show Up: Bigger & Bolder, Level Up: Make Boss Moves, and Alt + Ctrl + Del. She has been a featured speaker for Called Two Inspire Women's International Empowerment Conference, Comeback Summit, and Power Up, and The Leadership Experience Tour, and Sister Leader Conference

Website: www.3eeeconsulting.com

Facebook: 3EEE Consulting

Instagram: 3eeeconsulting

Email: 3eeeconsulting@gmail.com

Take the Mask Off: Find Purpose and Peace!

MIRIAM MATTHEWS

"Your legacy BEGINS where your mask ENDS and PEACE comes with being in your purpose!" -Miriam Matthews

"Oh no, I missed my period!" It was July 2010, during which I was enjoying the summer as best as I could, with one more year left of undergrad at Georgia State University. I was dating a guy, who wasn't my prince charming, but I had deemed him better than the "situation" I had been in right before him. The situation before him wasn't a good situation whatsoever, as the relationship was with someone twice my age who initially positioned himself as a mentor in my life. I wanted to get out of that toxic relationship so badly that instead of moving toward what I really needed (God), I focused on getting away from what I was experiencing and ended up in a similar relationship. However, this time he was around my age. We'd been dating on and off for less than a year. I always had questions about whether he'd been faithful, and later learned he wasn't. There had been many red flags that I'd ignored. Nevertheless, my self-esteem was so low that I attracted what I thought I deserved. I hardly knew myself and had been wearing a mask for years. July 2010 was also the same month when I realized that I missed my period. The pregnancy test that I decided to take was positive. My mother had been looking at me strangely for a few days as if she already knew. In the multitude of my thoughts, I began to desperately examine my decisions: "How did I get here? What am I going to do? What will my church and friends think of me? I'm going to have to hide this for as long as I can!" It was as if this examination would hopefully lead me to a solution of how to undo what I've done. I wanted these very uncomfortable feelings and thoughts to disappear, but they didn't.

Finally, my mom asked me in her Ghanaian accent, "Mimi, did you miss your period?"

Before I continue, let me tell you more about 2010. The year 2010 wreaked havoc on my resiliency and hope for a good future. My father became sick and moved from Georgia to North Carolina, to live with his sister. My parents had been divorced since I was a toddler. She invited him to stay, so he could receive some support. I had no idea what was to come in March 2010. One evening, while in my dorm room, I received a sudden phone call from my brother, who began to vehemently repeat, "Mimi, Daddy died!" I may have uttered the word "Whatttt?," in disbelief. Afterward, I remember just being speechless, as I began to cry. As tears rolled down my face, my roommates began to inquire about what had happened. I could offer no explanation until later, as I began to self-soothe and calm down. His funeral then occurred within the next 2 weeks. I forced myself to keep going and put more time and attention into the not-so-great relationship I had at the time.

Approximately 2 months later I was informed that my grandmother had passed away. My grandmother had just returned to Ghana in 2008 after living with us in Georgia since one of my brothers and I were born. She literally came here to help my mother raise us! For years, she poured into us. Although she was 88 years old when she returned to Ghana, we didn't anticipate that her passing would happen when it did. The death of a loved one is one of those things that you can't really be prepared for, even though you know it's inevitable, especially given her age.

Two consecutive losses. I felt reckless and certainly underestimated the needs of my emotional health.

Fast forward to July, I stood in the doorway unsure of what to say to Mom. Her question felt surreal. I thought, "Is my mom really asking me this right now?" Nevertheless, I had known for a couple of weeks and had already become heavy with keeping this news to myself. I took a deep breath and told her the truth with much uncertainty about the outcome. She stood in disbelief. "Oh, Mimi!" I became defensive and quickly acted as if I had things figured out. "I'm exploring my options!" I exclaimed. Her disbelief quickly turned into compassion and support. "Keeping the baby is best, Mimi."

The intense feeling of disappointment began to sink in. What would my father and grandmother be thinking? What does God think of me? As tears fell from my eyes, I felt like I let everyone down. Years of people-pleasing behavior and seeking outside validation, as a result of experiencing sexual trauma at age six, had really reared their ugly head this time. My constant seeking for love, validation, and repeated failed relationships were the opposite of the person I was in my church community and friendships. The dichotomy of my life hit a dead end. Before this, Mimi was a poster child, and I liked that! Sexual trauma doesn't happen to poster children, so I could act like it didn't happen. Inappropriate relationships don't happen to poster children, so I lived this dichotomous lifestyle. I'd been wearing a mask. I'd hide behind that mask because the idea of Mimi was accepted and liked at my church and other places, so I made sure to protect the idea of her. It wasn't until "Mimi" became pregnant out of marriage that I could no longer hide behind the mask anymore.

Let me tell you that there are some life challenges and decisions that will literally put you in a position that forces you to face your past, problems, and fears of persecution! I realized that it was my own judgment and mask that was killing my purpose. My pregnancy, though untimely and not under the preferred circumstances, was the driving force behind beginning to retire my mask and focus on my future. I was forced to confront my negative beliefs that created my low-self-esteem. And though I experienced the significant losses of my father and grandmother, I realized that they lived their lives. I had to decide how I was going to live mine and it was time to get to know the real me!

Your purpose requires that you take your mask off. Your purpose demands your authenticity. Many times, we're hiding or carrying shame due to what happened to us, what we've lost, or decisions we've made. However, let me tell you about the God I serve. I serve a God that says, "He loved us and died for us, while we were yet sinners." I realized I didn't have to do anything to get his unconditional love, and he truly wanted me and wants you to experience all of it! His love heals all wounds. His love grants you the permission to truly get to know yourself in the most authentic way through him. Connecting and deepening my relationship with God gave me the courage to take the mask off! After all, we're made in his image, and he tends to use the most "unlikely" individuals in UNFATHOMABLE MIRACULOUS WAYS! Won't He do it?

Romans 8:18 says, "I consider that our present sufferings are not worth comparing with the glory that will be revealed in us." Even though we experience trials and tribulations, there's a promise that glory will be revealed! I came to tell you that the tribulation or trial will not break you!

Even Job, who was a righteous and upright man, faced immense persecution and lost EVERYTHING! He was sick, and lost all his children, and his cattle! Though Job struggled emotionally and physically, he maintained his connection to God. He didn't understand why it was happening. All he knew was that it was "beyond" what he could fathom.

The enemy literally wanted the attack and affliction to disconnect Job from God. He wanted to prove he was no longer faithful to God after the experiences of death and loss of dignity. He wanted Job to forget about God, and who he is in God. If Job did this, he would have been abandoning where his identity is found. Loss of identity, or not knowing who you are in God leads to the mask. However, Job remained faithful despite his losses. Because of God's goodness and mercy, he received DOUBLE of everything he lost! Because he trusted God through the process, God gave and trusted Job with more!

Many times, we wouldn't know how resilient we are until we've been through a challenge. And if it wasn't for the challenge, we wouldn't experience the necessary change needed to get us out of our comfort zone. No matter the problem, I challenge you to see it as an opportunity in which God is preparing you for your assignment. Every problem that I've faced and overcome has equipped me to touch and help others heal and rise to their calling. A soldier wouldn't be prepared for battle if they've never experienced the grueling sweat, pain, and lessons that come with training. The trials that you face are training you for future victory! How? Because greater is he that is in you, than he that is in the world! Rise up, soldier! No longer do you need to remain stagnant in fear of what may happen. No longer do you need to analyze why this or that happened to you, to the point that your questions cause you to not answer the call on your life!

The key is to plug into Jesus Christ, which is plugging into his passionate love, peace, and purpose for you! He's passionate about you and your ability to move forward in your purpose! Jeremiah 29:11 says, "For I know the plans I have for you," declares the Lord, "plans to prosper you and not to harm you, plans to give you hope and a future." Your future is bright my friend. "Your legacy begins where your mask ends!"

It's time to recognize who you are in God, so you can persevere through every problem! Your purpose is waiting to be ignited, and it's time to take the mask off!

Miriam Matthews is a mom, wife, speaker, therapist, and a Christian transformational life coach! I always knew that I wanted to help others and that God has planted me in my passion for His glory! I am passionate about working with courageous, Christian women, who want to build their foundation on God and overcome fear! We are meant to dominate and create, and I believe that we carry the DNA of Christ inside of us. I'm the CEO of Define your DNA Coaching Academy where we dive into God, neutralize negative beliefs, and activate power and purpose! We all need support and accountability, and I challenge you to come and claim your inheritance! For help with processing your past to push towards your purpose, visit my website: www.define-your-dna.com, or complete a contact form by visiting bonus.defineyourdna.com!

Facebook: Miriam Matthews

Instagram: defineyourdna

Stand Strong through Perseverance and Find Inner Peace

MARWIN STRONG

"After every dark day it's a brighter day."

Tupac Shakur

What happens if you don't know if you will ever have a brighter day because your whole life has been dark? It's a question many of us are going through. Some have hardships, divorce, low self-esteem, abuse, alcoholism, being molested, depression, anxiety, loss of a loved one, you got the bad news from the doctor that you have been diagnosed with a disease you were not aware of, and many things that have been haunting you since you were a little child.

Growing up I faced hardship. My mother raised eight children by herself, and she had to do what she had to do to make sure her children had food and clothing and a place to lay their heads. My sisters and brothers were surviving and trying to live the best we knew how and at times our electricity, gas, and water would be shut off temporarily. There were times we did not have hot water, we had to go knock on the neighbor's door with a pot of water in our hand and ask, "Is it ok to use your stove to heat up this water so we can take a warm bath?"

I was the fourth child out of eight of my mother's children. I was the kid that was charming to get my way, sneaky, a class clown in school, always getting into something, and always in trouble, being a product of my environment living in the inner city where drugs and violence were a normal thing, watching people get murdered, prostitution, as I am hearing gunshots all through the day and night.

I was a good basketball player, which kept me away from the reality I was living. I spent most of my time staying on the basketball court in the projects. I had dreams of going to the National Basketball Association to play against the great Michael Jordan, my role model. I tried to mimic him and his Airness as he flew through the sky slam dunking on his opponents, fade away jumpers, and making last-second buckets.

I wanted to get my mother out of the neighborhood we lived in. I wanted to be rich, and for my mother to have her dream home, her luxurious car, living the life of other families we called "High-class citizens." The dreams I had were not the reality I had when I woke up because I was still in the same place I was before I went to sleep. I woke from a good dream to the bad reality of struggling to try to figure out, "Who am I? Will be anything in life? Will I live to be a teenager? As I have watched people die by guns, some of my closest friends I play basketball with at the playground are now in their graves from senseless violence."

I finally grew up, graduated from high school, became a great basketball player and my name started being noticed around my community and other states for my basketball skills. I had the opportunity to finally get that chance to go to the National Basketball Association. I played in a tournament in Indianapolis, Indiana. Every year professionals come from all over the country to play in the summer pro league tournament. I was invited to play in the tournament. The team I played on made it to the championship game as I was excited for this opportunity to one day meet my idol Michael Jordan and play against him. We won the championship game. I was awarded the most valuable player of the tournament and was invited to a try-out as a free agent to play professional basketball and get my mother her dream home. I dreamed about growing up.

I was excited about this once-in-a-lifetime opportunity so many other kids around the world desire just like I did when I was a young child. I decided I want to celebrate with my friends the great accomplishment I received. I went to a party to drink and have a good time because where I am from people do not make it out, they either die or are in prison.

We were dancing, had a great time drinking, smoking marijuana, and listening to '90s music with some of the most beautiful women I have ever seen in my life, dancing and buying each other drinks to see who we could take home after the party was over. As I was dancing with this lady I had my eye on, I finally got my opportunity. Someone handed me a drink and I drank it and it had poison in it. They spiked my drink to kill me because they were jealous of the accomplishment I achieved.

Tragedy came to me once again. Everything I worked for my whole life came to an end. I went home not knowing what was going on with my body but for days and weeks I was losing weight, my hair falling out, and my skin was turning different colors because the poison was destroying my internal organs. According to my mother, she found me in the bathroom having a scizure and they rushed me to the hospital. I was in a coma for a month. Doctors had a meeting and explained to them that I may not make it through the night as I lay in intensive care helpless while my vital signs were slowly declining. I was told if I came out, I would be a vegetable, meaning "other nurses and family members will have to assist you because you could not have the mobility to do it on your own."

My dreams of playing professional basketball were over. No more dreams of meeting Michael Jordan, no more running up and down the court. I was fighting to live with tubes all in my body, trek in my neck to help me breathe. I was lying in the hospital bed still in a coma and suddenly, I awoke and so many people were astonished by my opening my eyes. The family rushed into my room crying, calling family members and friends on thc phones in the joy that I woke up.

Though I woke up I had a long road ahead of me with the fear of slipping back into the coma, doctors giving me the bad news that I would never walk again, and a speech impediment. For two years I remained in the hospital going through speech therapy, physical therapy, and occupational therapy, like a newborn baby unsure of the outcome of my condition. I cried many nights in the hospital. I was hearing "code blue," which means someone has died and they must rush to their rooms so the doctors can perform cardiopulmonary resuscitation known as C.P.R.

After extensive rehabilitation, I walked out of the hospital after two years and went to play basketball in Boston, Massachusetts at the University of Massachusetts-Boston on a basketball scholarship. I continue to pursue my education with my degrees from Ivy Tech Community College and Ball State University. I started my not-for-profit organization called "Fight Against Drugs and Violence, Enough Is Enough Movement" to deter gun violence among young children around the world. I was awarded "The Star Press of the Year" for my efforts in my community to keep it safe and was honored to be a greeter in my hometown to welcome Ex-President Barack Obama to the city I lived in. I continue to accomplish goals by being the first and youngest African American Delaware County Building Commissioner, national motivational speaker, author, licensed elder, and author, and will be filming a movie called *Back from the Shadow of Death* from the book I wrote about my life growing up with biblical principles.

Remember it is light at the end of the tunnel. you cannot stop, you must persevere, do not give up, do not throw in the towel, stay strong and I guarantee you will overcome your adversity. The trials and tribulations that I went through taught me lessons that I share with the world. My passion is serving others and my purpose is to teach, preach, and reach everyone that you care enough to be all you can be and live in your divine assignment. This will lead to inner peace which will impact the people around you in a positive way.

Marwin Strong was born in the small, rural town of Muncie, Indiana. He is an author, motivational speaker, teacher, and elder. Marwin grew up in an inner-city neighborhood rife with poverty, drugs, violence, and discrimination. After a near-fatal attack by an unknown assailant, Marwin made a dramatic comeback from his former life by starting his own in-the-trenches war against drugs and violence. His experiences in the streets, and his unique speaking style due to his trauma, help him communicate with those in the community as well as those still in the drug game.

With frequent frustration, but also courage and hope, Marwin shows this kind of transformation can happen to anyone. Though his experience is told from a uniquely Christian perspective, Marwin's is a story for any person, from any religion, even for those who claim no religion at all. It is a story of hope for an America ravaged by overdoses from the opioid epidemic, suicide, homicide, and depression. Marwin Strong promises achieving dreams is possible for everyone, though he admits it will not be easy. With his unique life and message, Marwin shows that moving into the light of self-fulfilling dreams and success is a choice and a journey worth making. His first book, *Back from the Shadow of Death*, was an Amazon Best Seller. The book is currently being made into a feature film. His next book *Back from the Shadow of Death Two* will be published this winter.

Facebook: Marwin Strong

Instagram: @marwinstrong

Six Steps to Journey to Your Truth

BRITTANY BROWNE

"Peace. It does not mean to be in a place where there is no noise, trouble or hard work. It means to be in the midst of those of things and still be calm in your heart." – Unknown

Imagine growing up with an absent father and witnessing your mother battle cancer and pass away. Getting married at the age of 22 to someone twice your age, resulted in numerous relocations across the country. Those are just a few pieces of my story. I am Brittany Browne, the mentality coach, and I am here to share how my passion for purpose led me to peace. I grew up in the small town of Concord in North Carolina. My mom raised my sister and me as our father was in and out of our lives. We knew him, but he wasn't present physically or financially. My sister and I are 18 months apart and we have an older brother that is 11 years older than me and ten years older than her. My mom had him at the age of 16, and my grandmother became his guardian while my mom went into the Army. As far as my socioeconomic status, I would say that my household was below middle class. When I was nine years old, I remember my mom being diagnosed with rheumatoid lupus. We came to learn that it was an autoimmune disease that causes joint pain and inflammation. As a child, you don't really know what it means or how it is going to impact your family; you can only sit back and see how things unfold.

Being the sole provider for our household, my mom NEVER missed work. Regardless of the pain she was in, she made a way to support us. Working in a hosiery mill where they made and packaged pantyhose or "stockings," you could say that her job was very hands-on. I remember one day, my mom called my sister into the room, and told us to bring her a knife because her shoulder was in so much pain that she wanted to cut it off. Think about the amount of fear and confusion we were feeling. You know how parents always say, "Do what I say!" But somehow, we knew that this request wasn't coming from someone who was thinking clearly. She was desperate for relief. We called our grandmother, my mom's mom, to come over. Luckily, she lived in a house behind us and there was a little path that connected our house to hers. She was there in minutes to console her and give her meds. They ended up calling the doctor to see if there were any other pain management options. Over the years, she learned how to manage her symptoms and make lifestyle changes to minimize the flare-ups. What I did not know was that this was a snapshot of what it was going to look like in the years to come when it came to my mother's health.

In 2011, my mother was then diagnosed with cervical cancer that resulted in a hysterectomy. Following that, we learned cancer had spread to her bladder in 2012 and she had to have her bladder removed and a urostomy placed 2012. At this time, we were optimistic that we would be in the clear and her tests would all come back in her favor. In early 2013, we received news that the cancer was now in her colon, and she ended up having to go back into surgery to get a colostomy bag. Keep in mind that she was still getting radiation and chemotherapy in the midst of this. She ended up having to go on leave from her job where she worked in a group home with special needs adults. My grandmother who was in her seventies is taking her to chemotherapy three times a week and has also become her full-time caregiver.

On Wednesday, October 2, 2013, I got the call that hospice was on the way to get her from my grandmother's house, and it wasn't long until she passed away. I was in my second semester of nursing school at the time at the University of Colorado in Denver. I flew back to North Carolina that Thursday to manage her funeral services that were to take place on Saturday. On Sunday, I was back in Denver because I had clinicals on Monday and Tuesday. My colleagues knew that I had just lost my mom and I would hear things like, "What are you doing back so fast? I don't know what I would do if I lost my mom," or "You're so strong, why not take some time off to grieve?" But honestly, what was I supposed to do? Life goes on and my mom wouldn't have wanted me to risk not finishing my degree. The way CU's nursing program was designed they could not guarantee placement into the classes or cohorts once you withdraw. Grieving looks different for everyone, but I believe that knowing who I was at the core was what allowed me to keep forging ahead.

I married a corporate executive at a very young age. His desire for advancement required a lot of relocating. In 2009 we moved to Denver, CO, and stayed for about 7 years, then to Las Vegas for almost 2 years and the final stop was in Orlando, FL. He supported me as I obtained my nursing degree, placed me into diverse populations, and had me in rooms with people who were where I was trying to go. He was everything my absent father was not. So here I am married to a man who is financially stable, and I have a promising career as a nurse. I am thinking I got this life thing figured out. In September of 2020, my 11-year marriage ended abruptly … the process took about 18 days to be exact. I reflected on my life: absent father, my mother is deceased, and the godmother whom i called grandma also passed away in 2017. Then God is like, "Oh wait take this divorce too" like it was the cherry on top of a hot fudge sundae. I mean… I do like cherries, but not in this case. It was then that I realized abandonment was my ordained fight because I kept experiencing loss in human form. The people closest to me, that knew the things I had experienced, could not grasp the fact that I just kept it moving. This is not to say that I wasn't hurting, but after looking over my life I realized that, even in the losses, I gained experience and strength.

When evaluating your experiences and piecing together all the things you've overcome, you can usually see recurring themes. Many of us are just waking up every day and not being active participants in our lives. When I say that, I mean that we do not take the time to catch on to trends and patterns that ultimately impact our mental, spiritual and emotional states. We are just going through the motions, working, paying bills, and taking care of our families. The reason a lot of people have a hard time finding peace or their purpose is that they aren't real with themselves. They are too busy trying to keep an image to satisfy their ego or trying to live out someone else's dream or expectations. People will pass away, and relationships will end, but if we spend so much time focusing on what we lost, we miss out on the things we have gained. New people will come into your life. New bonds and relationships will be cultivated.

After my divorce in September of 2020, there was this need to know who Brittany really is? What does she want? What does she need? Still to this day, I do not know where the drive or the inspiration came from, but it was necessary. I created an interactive guide called "Supernova: Becoming the Star of Your Own Galaxy." This resource outlines six steps to reconnect with who you are in order to get what you want out of your life. It also helps you sort out patterns in your behavior that hinder you from seeing the light you have within.

The first step is Self-Discovery: Take the scenic route. What interests do you have? What did you want to be when you grow up? Are you doing that? What do you enjoy doing in your free time? What do you worry about the most? The next step is Self-Awareness: Who in the world are you? This step helps you find connectedness in the world around you. What do you like about your personality? What do others say about you? Do you agree with them? Are there things in society that trigger you? If so, do you know why? Step three is Self-

Acceptance: Who do you think you are? Do you practice positive self-talk? Do you equate your worth with your achievements, love life, or social status? You shouldn't, as these are all temporary. You must believe in your uniqueness and that there's no one else in the world like you. The fourth step is Self-Love: Evaluate the costs, but never negotiate your value. Can you create boundaries with others when you may be being taken advantage of? Are you able to understand your emotions without putting yourself down for responding to certain situations in a certain way? Step five is Transparency versus Truth. Transparency is the ability to express the details of an experience from your perspective, but Truth is different because there are multiple sides to a story. It is impossible for one party to recall every aspect of an event. It is not saying that you are wrong when you share your side of the story, but more of a way to say that you can be right and wrong at the same time. Is there a situation where you didn't get to tell your side of a story and you have been carrying that around? You should write it down how you remember it and tell your side of the story there; this then leads us to the final step: The Release. Let go of old ways of thinking. Let go of things you can't control. Let go of society's expectations and embrace every inch of your being.

As this chapter comes to an end, how well do you know yourself? How connected are you to your truth? It takes courage, wisdom, and compassion to fully accept the good, the bad, and the ugly. There can be no peace without truth. Everyone's purpose and journey are different, but we create a better way of living when we use what we have endured being of assistance to others. In understanding this, our perspective and approach to adversity change; if that lesson is yours to be learned, there is no running from it. Heartbreak and loss didn't kill me, it forced me to create something that could bring someone else out of the darkness. This is my passion; therefore, I know now that I am living in my purpose. As a result, I have inner peace. You can find it too. Learn from your trials and tribulations. Discover your passion and you can live in your purpose.

Brittany Browne is an educator, advocate, bestselling author, motivational speaker, and highly sought-after certified master life coach known for inspiring and delivering practical coaching methods to women across the world. She works with clients in discovering and defining both their personal and professional purpose to achieve goals and unlock the secrets to their own happiness. Through her work, Brittany gained the professional clarity in knowing that no two persons are the same, and to facilitate growth and transformation, coaching requires personalized, relatable, and uncanny approaches. Her down-to-earth style is one of the many traits most appreciated by her clients and is what sets her apart from others in her field.

Through her own past traumas and implementing the work required to rebuild,

Brittany has firsthand experience in helping people. Faced with rebuilding her own life while obtaining a nursing degree, she learned the deep internal work required for self-preservation. This work gave birth to a newer, brighter version of herself, leading to the development of Brittany Browne Life Coaching. Her services emphasize the power of connecting your past to your purpose and embracing your truth to cultivate meaningful connections within yourself and others. Because she found her light within, her intentions to help people find their light and to keep their light shining are not only rewarding but necessary.

Facebook: Brittany Browne

Instagram: iambrittanybrowne

A Dream Realized

MARIA THORPE

"Develop a passion for learning. If you do, you will never cease to grow." Anthony J. D'Angelo

As the youngest girl of eight children, I was exposed to many opportunities early in my life. I spent a lot of time with my eldest sister. Many thought my sister was my mother because I was always with her. She was 18 years older than me hence why some thought I was her daughter. I had a huge extended family too, consisting of aunts, uncles, nieces, nephews, and cousins, lots of cousins. However, trying to find my place, my purpose and my peace was not always easy. When I was growing up, I had lots of big dreams and I also had a lot of desires. We were not a rich family but we had what we needed to live a thankful life and that included lots of love.

Being part of a large family meant you did not always have quiet or time to be alone. Finding a place where I could think and figure things out could be difficult at home. As I got older, I sought out a place where I could dream, think and make plans. I would try to go to my room but inevitably one of my siblings would be there or show up shortly after my arrival. I would try using the kitchen but there was always someone coming in to get something to eat. I even tried the bathroom but needless to say, that was no good.

Eventually, after a lot of searching one of my older cousins suggested I go to the library. I asked which one. I guessed the one at school, but I was confused because that library always had students and sometimes it was crowded. They said, no, the *big* one. I recall saying, "The big one" with a weird look on my face. The free library of Philadelphia. It was awesome, huge, and full of my favorite thing, books! This place turned out to be my place of solace. I was blessed to have the largest library in the area within walking distance from my home, just one mile away. That place was my pretend mansion. I could go into the stacks to get quiet or a room with tables and windows to gaze out and look at the trees.

This place at this time in my life provided all that I needed to begin to create the life that I felt I desired. I was able to think, make plans, and have peace and quiet. I would visit as often as I could, after school, on weekends, and during the summer. This place allowed me to grow and learn about different places that I hope to visit one day. When I was there, I believed that I could do and be anything I wanted. Going to the library could change my attitude if I was having a bad day or something did not go my way. Having a positive attitude helped to make my dreams come true. In that building, I discovered my passion for learning, and I set my goal of going to college and making something out of my life.

I was grateful that I lived in a home where we were taught that education was key, and knowledge is power. Even though my mom did not graduate from high school, she knew the value of education. It was important to her that all of her children graduated from high school, and we all did. However, I wanted more. My time in the library had shown me there was a great big world out there and I was destined for greater things. My teachers and mentors introduced me to opportunities that open my eyes and various doors. After being introduced to Philadelphia Regional Introduction for Minorities to Engineering (PRIME) program, I knew what I wanted to do. I was going to be the first in my family to go to college for engineering. No one in my immediate family had accomplished this, but I had family and mentors who believed in me. I had the aptitude and the grades, and I was determined to pursue my passion.

My challenge was I did not have the money to go to college, but I was not going to let that deter me. I recall sitting in church one Sunday and praying for a solution to my problem. I remember my mother saying, "God helps the child who helps themselves." That quote motivated me to go to my quiet place and put together my strategy for success. My plan was to apply to colleges that had an accredited engineering program and get a scholarship that gave me enough to pay for my education. So I began that process. First, making sure that the university had the program I wanted to go to college; that they had funds/scholarships at the level to support my needs; and had a good rate of graduation for their students. This process helped me obtain several opportunities, each with its own possibilities for me to be successful.

This process and strategy I created allowed me, over my years, to obtain multiple degrees and training without having to pay for most of them. This process helps me find my passion. I was looking for whatever I chose to focus on. I did it with all my heart and put my mind to it. I put a plan in place that could create the desired outcome. During this process, a quote from Margaret Young came to mind:

"You must first be who you really are, then do what you need to do, in order to have what you want."

Margaret Young

During some of my most difficult times, I was able to go to my quiet place, again and again, where I could think, plan and come up with a solution. My strategy worked and my plan came into view. I obtained multiple scholarships offers that paid for my education, books, tuition, and room and board. This allowed me to continue my dream of getting my degree in engineering.

As I went forward to get my degree, I had several trials and tribulations. The major one was the loss of several key loved one. It began with my dad, then my mom, my aunt, and my brother. There were so many times I thought about giving up. But I thought, what would this accomplish? During times of chaos and stress in our lives, like homelessness, sickness, and loss of loved ones, we must find ways to create, find or keep our inner peace because it will help us to continue to move in the direction of our purpose.

As I have gotten older and wiser, I find it most important to find time for yourself each day. "Me time" is time for you to do things you love, and have a passion, that gives you energy, makes you happy, and fill fulfilled. Also, during "my" me time I want to shut out the noise and be still. I still love finding that quiet place where I can think and find solutions to problems that I may be having, and to de-stress.

In conclusion, here are my five simple steps for finding peace in my daily life. I hope you can use them to bring peace to your day.

1. Morning meditation and prayer.

2. Take time to exercise, at a minimum I plank each day for a minute.

3. Take time to learn something new no matter what it is. Expanding your mind will keep your problem-solving skills in top shape.

4. Taking time to smell the flowers for me on some days means having a conversation with an old friend or enjoying a walk in nature.

5. Finally, take time to be grateful. It is so easy to complain about what you don't have, so why not use that same time to be grateful for what you do have.

One of my daily mantras is to remember to dream, believe, and achieve so you can receive and live inside your passion, work on your purpose and create a place of peace.

Today I am so grateful that I am able to give back to my community and my family by sharing my story as a Black female in STEM and the things I have learned along my journey. One of the ways I share my passion is I mentor groups of young ladies, in local schools, where I teach them how to find their purpose through four pillars of success. I teach them to know themselves, to dream big, and how to overcome obstacles and take action. This helps them to find their purpose. Another area I can share is through the co-ownership of the Waldorf Chess Club, Inc., with my husband. Here we teach youth how to strategically think and plan, as well as build confidence through the game of chess. Both activities help me to create a place where youth can find some inner strength and peace. I will leave you with this simple daily strategy that can work towards solving both small and large issues. Use my three Ps of success: live in your purpose, make a plan, and be persistent until you get the outcomes you desire.

"If you are depressed, you are living in the past. If you are anxious, you are living in the future. If you are at peace, you are living in the present." Lao Tzu

Maria Thorpe currently works for the Federal Government in engineering. She is an international bestselling author, speaker, mentor, and real estate agent. She has mentored numerous students and professionals in Science, Technology, Engineering, and Math (STEM). She has spoken at various events, including local organizations, schools and colleges inspiring girls and empowering women, sharing with them how they can be the best with the gifts and talents that God gave them.

Ms. Thorpe is the co-owner of Waldorf Chess Club Inc., which she founded with her husband. She works with children as young as five, helping them find their inner strength, hone their decision-making skills, and build confidence through the game of chess. Ms. Thorpe is a graduate of Pennsylvania State University with a Master of Engineering, Engineering Science degree and a graduate of Drexel University, Philadelphia, PA with a Bachelor of Science in Electrical Engineering. She has received numerous awards and honors including 2021 Maryland Mother of the Year.

Facebook: Maria Thorpe

Unlock and Unleash your Passion Purpose and Peace

DR. BETTY B. SPEAKS

"Love life. Engage in it. Give it all you've got. Love it with a passion because life truly does give back, many times over, what you put into it." – Maya Angelou

My name is Betty Burroughs Speaks and I often ask leaders "Are you leaving A Lifetime IMPRINT?" I am very passionate about educating others on maneuvering through the pathway of their trials and tribulations by engaging their passion, purpose, and peace. As the founder of The Resurrection Imprint ACT, I introduce a new paradigm that one needs to resurrect in after experiencing life's misfortunes and if one resurrects in the right way, one leaves an Imprint for Infinity. After all, leadership is all about others, inspiring them to believe, then empowering that belief to become reality. Inside each of us is a "Resurrection of passion, purpose, and Peace (imprint act)." We just need to learn how to unlock and unleash them.

Another passion of mine is motivating others! I start out asking them "Are You MOTIVATED!" Their response would be "Motivated, motivated, downright motivated, you check us out! You check us out hooah." I would then ask them to chant, "I am someone SPECIAL, uniquely created by God! Greatness is within me, and I am full of POTENTIAL."

I served as a senior non-commissioned officer in the United States Army on both friendly and unfriendly grounds. My most traumatic encounter was the TERRORIST attack at Khobar Towers in Saudi Arabia. Just think for a second! It's over 100 degrees outside and your heart's desire is to cool off by taking a nice cool shower. The moment you feel that water against your body you are lunged out of the shower with a force of hot fragments that are bursting through your bathroom window. I strongly believe that God kept me so that I could share my story with others so that they too can find peace and resurrect in their pain. *Psalm 4:8: "In peace I will lie down and sleep, for you alone, LORD, make me dwell in safety."*

Nearing the age of 47, I became debilitated because of challenging hallucinations, nightmares, and anxiety attacks, due to life disappointments including deployment on military hostile assignments. I was blind to the option of having an indisputable disorder, I ignored the warning signals [crying in my sleep, waking up from nightmares, not being able to fall asleep, avoiding crowds, loud noises, people walking up on me without my knowing, etc.]. I shut completely down when someone betrayed me. For over a decade, I encountered, endured, or reminisced one nervous fear after the other. There was 9-11 and its tributaries, several incidents on military installations, several horrific incidents at high schools, colleges, and elementary schools, and even an explosion at my last employment (UMASS Lowell) including a car explosion in front of our home, several community events (Boston Bombing). I attempted to suppress my pain and fears by avoiding (people, places, TV, radio etc.). However, I became easily irritated, with a very low tolerance of non-sense and impatience; agitation and unacquainted aggravations will literally ignite an outburst of unforeseen belligerence, it does not matter to whom or the location. I often go into isolation in fear of what might happen next; this has been disturbing. Bottom line is that I needed professional care and I didn't know whom to notify nor did I know how to seek help.

As a result, I attempted to take my life by driving off a bridge that I crossed over nearly every day. That night it was no more issues to tissue, I felt nothing, nor no one, just wanted it all to go away. Then suddenly my SUV was stopped by a neighborhood rescue vehicle who had just finished an emergency call and noticed that I was driving unsafely on the bridge, and somehow manage to awake me from my daily thoughts of driving off that bridge. I didn't seek help because I felt as though I had to continue to set the example for my siblings and for my soldiers, being that I was a senior non-commissioned officer for the United States Army.

"We may encounter many defeats, but we must be undefeated" is one of my favorite quotes by Maya Angelou

So, when I was diagnosed with post-traumatic stress disorder (PTSD), I felt ashamed, mute, and embarrassed. I initially couldn't accept my diagnosis because I had been trained to lead and to take care of my soldiers and their wellbeing, not to mention I was an accomplished soldier. I was concerned that others would label me as being crazy or not accept me at all. Having a stress disorder was draining, like Super Woman having her powers taken from her. If you can imagine kryptonite debilitating Superman's strength, which of course made him an easy target to his enemy, that's how I felt with post-traumatic stress disorder. I didn't want to end my LIFE; I wanted to end the pain of hopelessness.

"God gives his toughest battles to his strongest soldiers." Ephesians 6:10–18

I will never forget the year, the date or the time. August 8, 2018, at 08:00 am (Year of the Great Eight). My women's health doctor personally telephoned me to inform me that I was detected with stage 3 cancer. To this day I am still in a state of shock. After having been on battlefields for my country, the battle of adjusting to life after the battlefield, and now the battle of cancer. I didn't cry but I WAILED until I couldn't share another tear! I am cancer-free today!

"Peace, I leave with you, My peace I give to you; not as the world gives do I give to you. Let not your heart be troubled, neither let it be afraid." John 14:2

Based on everything I have shared with you thus far; is why one will often hear me say that death came upon me three times on my journey in life. Each time the Holy Spirit interfered reminding me that I was chosen to live and not die. Reminding me that I still had several missions to accomplish that would leave an imprint on the lives of others "Worldwide" who were chosen to lead. Additionally, for more than 200 years women have been Impacting Changes in the world. The song that I recorded ("It's A Resurrection"), remains an opportunity to give my testimony from a leader's reflection as that wise woman I can conquer my passion walk in my purpose, and be at peace, as I embraced my pathway through trials and tribulations.

This allowed me to resurrect to lead because He's alive me. Therefore, I am wholehearted and grateful to Psalm Ebube featured artist by way of Lagos, Africa. Psalm did a phenomenal job composing and singing.

Leadership is a role that I am too familiar with therefore I opted to live my LIFE as a lifetime IMPRINT Leader!

So, today what helps me is speaking, teaching and most of all still serving and leaving impactful imprints.

~ John Wicker said that ***"Opportunities multiply as they are seized, they die when neglected."***

For the most part, we all face some form of trauma in our LIFE and as a leader, I love sharing opportunities that have worked to help me personally to resurrect and leave a personal and professional IMPRINT on another's life! I am extremely passionate about empowering individuals to resurrect and establish themselves through the four components of LIFE (Spiritual Growth, Financial Literacy, Personal Development, and professional development). I am that chosen warrior who inspires others to create an IMPRINT that will live on long after they're gone.

"When you wish someone joy, you wish them peace, love, prosperity, happiness... all the good things." Maya Angelou

Inspiring others to SOAR with H.O.P.E

> **S.O.A.R** Seize Opportunities and Resurrect **S.O.A.R** Seize Opportunities and Refocus
>
> **H.O.P.E** Help Other People Excel **H.O.P.E** Help Other People Enjoy Life
>
> **H.O.P.E** Help Other People Every day

Because this defines being at peace

"When you wish someone joy, you wish them peace, love, prosperity, happiness... all the good things." Maya Angelou

As an I Change Nations Global Civility ICON, my purpose is to help you resurrect your dreams and help you create the imprint that you envision leaving in this world for its eternity. Steve Jobs, the co-founder of APPLE, quoted it best .... by saying that, "Our time is restricted, so don't waste it living someone else's life. Don't be trapped by others' beliefs which are living with the results of other people's thinking. Don't let the noise of others' opinions drown out your own inner voice. And most importantly, have the courage to follow the direction of your heart plus your instinct." Leadership is not about titles, and status, is all about others, inspiring them to believe, then abetting that belief to become reality. A leader is anyone who takes responsibility for recognizing the potential in people and ideas and has the courage to resurrect those potentials. Resurrection Communication

– constantly connecting with others, because today more than ever the leader in both the messenger and the message

Listen – breaking down the executive ladder to gather insights at all levels—mostly what the leader doesn't want to hear (TRUTH)!

Learn – applying learning agility, to "know what to do when you don't know what to do."

Lead – empowering others in a bottom-up culture that is more nimble, agile, innovative, and entrepreneurial than ever before.

Only by embracing these truths can leaders master the resurrection imprint act that will completely disrupt a business landscape.

Have you ever tried to make a change for the better in your life?

3 Action steps to begin Leaving Your LIFE IMPRINT as a Leader.

1. Assess your experiences in LIFE, then concentrate on your greatest strengths and your most fulfilling experiences.

Questions to ask yourself:

• What do I naturally gravitate towards? (Something that you genuinely want to share) remembering that leaders genuinely lead

• What pain or experience do I not want others to experience? (Experience you overcame that you don't want others to suffer from)

What makes me feel awesome? (In a state of flow)

These experiences may smack you in the face with your LIFE purpose or give you hints.

You never know, but you'll need to REFLECT on to RESURRECT.

Secondly, Assess where you're at right now in LIFE. What resonates with you? For me it's inspiring others to rise above the unknown life challenges

You have likely changed over the past few years. There may be a specific reason why you are currently right here right now.

Maybe because it didn't resonate with you, so observe those differences and get ready to resurrect.

Your job is to connect the dots from your past experiences in LIFE, to what truly resonates with you right now.

Lastly, take action. Confirm or deny what resonates with you and empower others of your LIFE journey IMPRINTS.

Remember, your RESURRECTION is already within you. You may use external resources to help you extract it. (Mentorship, Mastermind)

What I want you to do is take a look at all your setbacks and tell yourself: I will Seize Opportunities and Rise above them (SOAR)

In Psalms 92:12, the Lord speaks about the palm tree. It's a palm tree that is planted and flourishes, the tree of Lebanon that still grows, one that still bears fruit despite the wind and the rains.

Rise above the storms.

Rise above the mental remnants of war and trauma.

Rise above domestic violence, sexual abuse, or divorce.

Rise above whatever you've gone through, whatever you need to resurrect from, knowing that God is still resurrecting each and every one of us.

One of my favorite quotes by Dr. Betty Speaks is that…

"Strong people are not simply born they RESURRECT by sharing IMPRINTS they generate throughout their life journey©."

Reminder, assess your LIFE experiences, assess where you are right now in LIFE, and take action by connecting with bettyspeaks.com.

I am Dr. Betty Speaks, and I am your IMPRINT CIVILITY LEADER because I empower others to resurrect and leave A Peaceful Lifetime IMPRINT.

Wise leaders inspire others to follow and believe in them and the calling of their mission by the presence of passion, partaking in humility, and being civil to all their encounters. ~ Betty B. Speaks

Constantly chant to yourself "I am someone SPECIAL,"

"Greatness is within me" and "I am full of POTENTIAL"!

I invite you and your friends to reach out to me at bettyspeaks.com. Under contact type in the word IMPRINT.

Dr. Betty B. Speaks is retired with HONORS from the United States Army. She is a unique one-of-a-kind scholar and initiator of The Resurrection Imprint Act. She is an award-winning I Change Nations International Ambassador, speaker, global network virtual marketer, and entrepreneur, eight-times bestselling author, Jesus Woman at Godheads Ministry, certified mastery storyteller, and certified black belt speaker plus she has been featured on TV shows and a host of radio broadcasting.

Dr. Betty B. Speaks is the CEO of A Life Change NOW, an Inspirational Speaker on Our Praise Christian Network TV in addition to being a sought-after Podcaster~ Host of Overcoming Battles by Being Strong and Courageous. The artist/Songwriter of the Single "It's A Resurrection." A genuine Royal IMPRINT EMPRESS! She is very passionate about MOTIVATING individuals to resurrect and establish themselves spiritually, personally, and professionally. She is known to be that chosen WARRIOR who INSPIRES others to create A Life Change Now by leaving an INTENTIONAL IMPACTFUL IMPRINT for INFINITY. Dr. Betty Speaks' influential messages are filled with positivity and encouragement. She inspires her audience in the use of their voices to speak the truth and to stand up for what is right.

Website: www.bettyspeaks.com

Facebook: Betty Speaks

Instagram: bettyspeaks

YouTube: Betty Speaks

What L.I.E.S Beneath?

CAROL CAMPBELL-FULLARD

"Remember, you don't have to be defined by your childhood trauma. You can start healing today." Samuel Zulu

"Our deepest fear is not that we are inadequate. Our deepest fear is that we are powerful beyond measure. It is our light, not our darkness, that most frighten us. We ask ourselves, who am I to be brilliant, gorgeous, talented, fabulous? Who are you not to be?" (M. Williamson). As my fingers circled and caressed the rim of my glass, I read those words once again more deeply than ever before. It felt as if I was reading them for the first time. Each word gripped and challenged me to walk more authentically in my being. I no longer needed to cower and dim this light to fit in. I needed exposure so that the fullness of what God intended for me could be revealed.

"Carol! You have a phone call!" I remember running to the phone with enthusiasm because someone was calling me. I quickly picked up the phone and immediately noticed my mother did not hang up. Clearly, she was trying to figure out who had called.

"Hello."

"Hello Carol."

"Yes?" I said in a quizzical tone trying to decipher the voice on the other end.

"This is Laura and I think it's time you met your little brother."

"Huh? What?" Before I could say another word, my mother screamed, "Carol hang up the flipping phone!" I hung up the phone bewildered and confused. I did not understand what was going on. I walked out of the room to a barrage of yelling. Words spewed from her mouth like a river breaking through a levee flooding the phone with curses and threats hurled at the unknown caller's voice. I watched her release anger and disdain like never before. She slammed the phone down, marched into her room, and began throwing my dad's stuff into bags and boxes. I looked at the surroundings and knew enough to stay out of her way and not ask any questions. She continued shuffling clothes and things everywhere. At some point, her adrenaline must have slowed because she calmly came into my room and asked if I was okay. I nodded my head yes and she hugged me tightly.

That night I was sent to bed earlier than usual. I tossed and turned in bed anxious about what was going to happen next when Daddy got home. Eventually, I heard the lock jiggling and knocking on the front door. "Open the door!" a voice yelled out. I peeked out of my bedroom to see my mother moving quickly past bags and boxes she organized near the door. She opened the door and with swiftness began throwing his things out while screaming about a woman calling her house about another child. Her voice shrieked as she continuously yelled, "Get out! Get out! Get out!" My father looked down the hall to see me crying as he got his things and left. It would be two weeks before I would see him again as he collected the rest of his belongings and said, "I love you." Now we were a family of two. It would take years to find peace in the trauma I experienced that day.

As I sat in the corner of my room, I was that eleven-year-old girl again watching my family change. I could feel my body rocking back and forth to shake off the hurt and anger. I pressed my head into my thighs and grunted out the pains, which soon turned into cries of helplessness. I beckoned for God, my parents—anything that would make this moment go away. Once again, I suffered humiliation and was broken. This time it felt so hard to get up and pull the pieces together. I willed myself to stand up and fight for my life, but nothing happened. I continued to sit, sob, and soak my shirt in tears. I eventually noticed that the light outside turned to dark and just like that, another day was beginning to disappear. I finally pulled myself up from the floor, crawled into the bed, and began to sift through my memories.

It was one thing to be betrayed as a child, but now I was walking in the same footsteps as my mother. A call. An argument. Another child was on the way and it was not mine. My only saving grace: we were not married. I was now a single parent, living in a new state, striving to combat painful feelings, and learning to control my moods. Just like that trauma of years past collided with the present and its heaviness was unbearable. I was stuck. How do I make peace with the past and present to live a fulfilling life?

Living in the past can rob your present and taint your future. The failure to forgive creates misery and prolongs negative thoughts. Being present meant I needed to find a way to forgive both myself and others. This was the only way to reclaim my life. As a single mother, I did not want these wounds to seep into the way I raised my child. She deserved better. My behavior would always be on display as an indication of how she should live her life. Giving yourself and others, the gift of forgiveness is not easy, but it is healing. Mahatma Gandhi said, “The weak can never forgive. Forgiveness is an attribute of the strong.” It was in the stages of forgiveness that I found both my strength and peace. I learned to pour into the students that walked across the threshold of my school each day. As I taught them to handle issues from a place of forgiveness and peace, I was reconciling my pain and creating a space for restoration.

Every hardship provides a lesson. We must determine the lessons learned from the experience. Moreover, pay attention to your mind and quiet the mental chatter that attempts to disrupt the peace you seek. Challenge those "thinking traps" and remember all the past issues you have survived. You are more than a conqueror!

Dr. Viktor Frankel states, "When we are no longer able to change a situation, we are challenged to change ourselves." Life will always be stressful. Our responses to hardship are habitual. Our habits can be altered or broken. One of the best habits a person can create is to become socially aware of how they are needed in the world. There is no greater peace than pouring into the lives of others. Those who need your hope, wisdom, and courage. This is a moment to create inner peace. This is a moment to "still the noise" and reach out in service to others. I promise that as you begin the heart work of bringing resources, resilience, and resolution to a community of people the power of reconciliation will once again manifest from within.

This is your moment to thrive as you bless others uncompromised. As you turn your pieces into peace always hold fast to what L.I.E.S beneath:

Love

Inspiration

Endurance

Strength

Carol Campbell-Fullard is a Certified Educator and ICF Professional Coach who works with individuals and organizations to develop successful breakthrough transformational strategies. She has worked with many clients to create and execute actionable success metrics to grow and expand their vision. Carol is a speaker and leadership facilitator who believes in leading from the "inside out." As an educational leader and coach, she offers a distinctive approach to meeting the needs of clients by uniquely positioning them to utilize emotional intelligence in order to disrupt inefficient patterns, so they become confident individuals and balanced leaders. Over the years shc has provided many innovative workshops including mindset shift, social-emotional wellness, developing vision, facilitating leadership and transformation, building teams as well as strengthening organizational culture and climate.

Carol received her bachelor's degree from Ithaca College, master's in Education from City University of New York Lehman College, and Executive Master's in Leadership from Georgetown University. She also holds both Advanced Professional Teacher and Administrator I and II Certifications. She is an Amazon Bestselling

Author of the books *Disrupt or Die: An Educator's Journey, Unmute Yourself and Unleash Your Undeniable Impact* with Dr. Cheryl Wood and Les Brown

Facebook: Carol C Fullard

Instagram: iammypieces

Discovering Purpose through Pain

Dr. Rhonda M. Wood

"For I know the plans I have for you,' declares the Lord, 'plans to prosper you and not to harm you, plans to give you hope and a future."

Jeremiah 29: 11, NIV

How many of us have experienced a challenge, difficulty, or some sort of struggle lately? May you have thoughts on "Why me? Why is this happening? Life is not fair! Nothing is going right." I remember a time a few years before the pandemic. I was at the height of my career. I had just started a dream job working full-time at a high-level corporate job at one of the most influential firms in the country. Like every professional, I dreamed of climbing the corporate ladder. And like every mother, I dreamed of a life full of love, laughter, and a bright future for my child. Then, one day my dreams drastically changed when my teenage daughter was diagnosed with depression, anxiety, and a mood disorder. Instead of the compassion and understanding I desperately needed during that challenging time in my life, I was shunned, abandoned, and looked down on. I was completely devastated, fighting through tears, and feeling the full weight of my situation on my shoulders.

Unsurprisingly, my daughter's mental health diagnosis bought my mental health challenges to the surface. There was no doubt that I was burned out and stressed, overwhelmed, discouraged, and unhappy. I battled with depression and anxiety every day. Most days it felt like they were winning. I woke up with them and drove to work with them. When I arrived at the office, they were right there waiting for me. Many times, I wanted to speak up, but it felt like depression and anxiety had their hands around my throat preventing me from saying a word. I also did not speak up for my mental health because I did not want to appear weak and was too afraid of what others may think. I remember believing that people with mental health symptoms did not look like me. In fact, experts say that many Black women feel they must project an image of invulnerability because the stigma around mental health deters them from seeking help. To that point, oftentimes, I was the only woman or person of color in corporate settings, and knowing how hard I fought to get there, I frequently felt the need to prove that I belonged there. Always striving to appear strong, in control, and in charge. But beneath the surface, I was slowly breaking down. My mental health was affecting my personal and professional life. It became too much trying to balance motherhood, mental health, and my career. I finally developed the courage to ask for help. I took a much-needed leave of absence from work and my daughter, and I prioritized our mental health through therapy sessions, support groups, and other resources. We also did move therapy, music therapy, and my personal favorite, movie therapy.

There was a classic movie in the '80s called *Karate Kid*. Now, there have been so many versions since then it is likely you have at least heard of it if you have not seen one of the remakes. In the movie, Daniel starts doubting if Mr. Miyagi really knows what he is doing. Why is Mr. Miyagi putting him through all these tasks? Does Mr. Miyagi not care about him? Is it even worth obeying? Often when we are hurting, we can start to ask the same sort of questions that Daniel asks in the film. We start to doubt. We are uncertain. We start to question. Things can seem hopeless. In the movie, Daniel wants Miyagi to teach him karate, but instead, Miyagi gets him to do a list of chores. Miyagi instructs him to "wax on, wax off," sand the floor and paint the fence. Daniel thinks he is being asked to do these things simply to earn the right to learn from Miyagi. Instead, all the while, Miyagi is teaching him karate without him even realizing it.

God works that way with us sometimes. God gives us little tasks and little callings, and if we are obedient to the smaller things, they become the stepping stones to a much greater purpose for our lives. Luke 16:10 says, "Whoever can be trusted with very little can also be trusted with much." We must learn to discern and obey God in the trivial things so that we can live our lives filled with His perfect purpose.

Most people are familiar with the verse Jeremiah 29:11, where it says, "'For I know the plans I have for you,' declares the Lord, 'plans to prosper you and not to harm you, plans to give you hope and a future.'" I do not think there is one Christian who does not hope to live a life of purpose. The problem is that many Christians are not willing to "wax on, wax off" to get there. In the verses following Jeremiah 29:11, God gives the "wax on, wax off" instructions, the key to unlocking His plans and purpose for us. Most people don't even read the verses that follow this well-known and overly quoted verse. In verses 12-14 it says, "You will call on me and come and pray to me, and I will listen to you. You will seek me and find me when you seek me with all your heart." Seeking God with all your heart is the key to unlocking His purpose for you. It means being obedient when God asks you to paint the fence and sand the floor. It means having the intentional resolve to obey and seek Him in the everyday ordinary so that you can live out His extraordinary purpose for you.

Have you ever wondered if there might be more? If God made you for more of a purpose than how you are living right now? Scripture is clear that He can do immeasurably more than all you could ever ask or imagine through Christ who lives in and through you (Ephesians 3:20-21). But you must be willing to walk before you fly.

"Sometimes the biggest move of God is wrapped up in the smallest acts of obedience." – Priscilla Shirer. And in addition, sometimes the best blessing, the best lessons, do not come wrapped in a big red shiny bow but instead may come packaged in unattractive packaging. So, what are you going to do today to show God you are willing to? I have listed three steps that will help you along the way to finding your purpose which will lead to inner peace.

1. TRUST THE (Divine) TIMING, it is a time like it or not. Whether you are in your 20's, 40's, or 60's, we are going to go through experiences that will never be convenient. It will always be a tough time. There are things that we desire or will go through that have already happened, are happening now, or have not happened yet. One scene in *The Karate Kid* shows Mr. Miyagi doing this very cool karate pose called the crane. Daniel asks Miyagi to teach it to him, but Miyagi simply tells him, "First learn stand, then learn fly." In other words, the steps are ordered. And we must trust the timing.

2. TRUST THE TRANSITION from one dimension to the next. The first stage is transformation. Daniel transitioned from being bullied and feeling sorry for himself to feeling empowered and standing up for himself. I transitioned from being too afraid to address my mental health issues to becoming an advocate for others and an international motivational speaker on mental health issues.

3. TRUST THE TRANSFORMATION (metamorphosis) renewing of the mind.

Daniel's transformation came about because he trusted the timing, the transition, and from being bullied to standing up for himself. I transformed myself into a confident, empowered woman who shares my message with the world through speaking on mental health issues. I know this is my purpose. I have a sense of inner peace, knowing through all the trials and tribulations, I found my purpose through the pain.

There will be a time when everything comes together, everything will make sense, and you will understand why it had to happen the way it did. You will look back on the experience and marvel at the strength you acquired along the way. Wondering how you ever made it through what was once thought to be a complicated situation. And most importantly you will understand why it had to be you.

Adversity is an inevitable part of life, and many people around the world are experiencing challenges from loss, pain, or heartbreak. These feelings can awaken a profound search for meaning and finding your purpose in your pain is an essential part of healing. Do not let the confusion of your pain cloud the clarity of the purpose it can serve in your life. I learned that certain experiences are meant to stretch and take us to greater heights. God uses our most painful experiences to produce our greatest purpose. They generate seeds of character, resilience, and strength that need to grow. As you navigate the detours, diversions, and disruptions of life, be sure not to let difficulties limit your ability to dream, experience joy, or make an impact in the world. Not only will you heal, but your example will also inspire others to do the same.

Dr. Rhonda M. Wood is recognized as one of the most prominent voices for mental health advocacy. Dr. Wood is an award-winning international keynoter, bestselling author, and a leading authority on mental health. Leveraging over 30 years of corporate experience, Rhonda impacts audiences with her mission to normalize and destigmatize mental health conversations. She trains audiences worldwide to eradicate mental health stigmas and adopt compassion, awareness, and acceptance.

Rhonda uses her unique voice and talents to serve women from the classroom to the boardroom. She unapologetically shares her mental health journey with a level of transparency that allows her voice to resonate in the hearts of women around the globe. In a world where women stay silent about mental health issues, Rhonda chooses to speak up on matters that have remained in the shadows. She has developed a deep-rooted passion for helping women reset their values, renew their vision, and rediscover their voices.

Recognized as a well-known fixture in her community, Rhonda works alongside decision-makers on improving the mental health system. She works tirelessly to raise mental health awareness and is an active member, volunteer, and presenter with the National Alliance on Mental Illness in Prince George's County. She serves as a parent advocate for transitional age youth as part of the Prince George's County Health Department System of Care. She is the founder of several programs, including "Laugh, Cry, Heal, ™" "Heal Out Loud, ™" and "Win from Within, ™" designed to help people heal emotional wounds and traumas to become happy, healthy, and whole.

Rhonda has received numerous awards for her leadership, commitment, and contributions to her community and the next generation. Her work has been featured on prominent media platforms such as ABC, NBC, FOX, CBS, talk shows, radio, podcasts, newspapers, magazines, and more.

Website: https://www.rhondamwood.com

Facebook: Dr. Rhonda M Wood

Instagram: Dr. Rhonda M Wood

LinkedIn: Dr. Rhonda M Wood

Twitter: Dr. Rhonda M Wood

Email: info@rhondamwood.com

Speaker Profile: https://speakerhub.com/speaker/dr-rhonda-m-wood

Afterword

Dr. Desziree Richardson

"Finally, brothers and sisters, rejoice! Strive for full restoration, encourage one another, be of one mind, live in peace. And the God of love and peace will be with you." 2 Corinthians 13:11

What a great quote to capture the chapters of this anthology. An anthology with stories of the bible, hope, purpose, passion, and peace. Each author brings another level of awareness to the possibility of inner peace by living in your purpose and fulfilling your divine assignment.

The visionary author, Dr. Theresa A. Moseley has complied 14 stories of trials and tribulations that eventually led to inner peace. The contributing authors recognized that using their gift to serve others, learning from the trials that life brings, and living in their purpose, bring inner peace. When everyone has inner peace, there is peace in the world. As I reflect on the stories of the co-authors, I realized how powerful these stories are. The foreword author Melissa Love set the stage by sharing biblical stories and the trials and tribulations of Joseph. Dr. Tasheka Green followed with more biblical stories while sharing her pain including the death of her mom who left her with an assignment. Dr. Green is fulfilling that promise and is living in her purpose. Marwin Strong has a story of hope, will, and purpose and he has discussed the trials and tribulations of living in Muncie, Indiana, and surviving death after two years in a hospital. Antonio Love found the love of his life and realized his wife ignites his passion. In his words, "purpose ignites passion, and delivers ultimate peace." Marteka was told she had breathing problems all her life and never participated in sports, only to find out that she could run around her neighborhood. A false narrative was created for Marteka on what she could or could not do. Marteka was resilient and found peace in her truth. Nadia Monsano discussed her transition from Trinidad to America where the cultures were different. She was bullied on a school bus just because the color of her skin was black. She had a wonderful teacher who demanded all students respect Nadia and her culture. However, it was her grandmother who told her to love herself and never change to fit in anywhere. Nadia is at peace with herself, knowing she is Black and beautiful. Dr. Rhonda Wood discusses how she turned her pain into purpose and now she is a sought speaker on mental health issues. Jayleen Ortiz and Brittany Brown described how they found their authentic self. Their truth set them free. Jayleen allowed others to create the narrative of who she was. Once she discovered her truth, it led to inner peace. As she states in her chapter, "I am the best version of me." Dr. Theresa's story is a clear example of no matter how bad situations are, no matter how many trials and tribulations you go through, there is a light at the end of the tunnel. Dr. Moseley was homeless for three days and woke up one morning realizing she owned two homes now, with twin Mercedes in her garage and a PhD in education administration. How does this happen? She discovered that all the solutions to her problems were already in her. The material things represented success and prosperity; however, she was NOT fulfilled until she started serving others, which lead to her inner peace. She discovered that life is about fulfilling your divine assignment by using your gift and passion. Her gift is her voice. Her passion is serving others. Her purpose is to make the world a more peaceful place. Dr. Onika Shirley and Joi Brown discussed God's plan for them. Carol

Campbell-Fullard showed us how she overcame childhood trauma to work with students in school and teach them to be their authentic self. Maria Thorpe shared her trials and tribulations of coming from a large family; however, she found peace in the library which started her trajectory to inner peace. Finally, Dr. Rhonda Wood brought everything together by stating trust in the transition and transformation. When you go through trials and tribulations in life and learn the lessons along the way, you will transform into what you were born to do on this earth. There you will find inner peace. The authors symbolize hope, passion, and propulsion that helps them escape their trials and tribulations. Through it all, they overcame, concur, and fulfilled their desires by sharing their journey here. Their stories connected deeply beyond the outer layer, which brought admiration. It was their inner strength and determination, along with a deep sense of gratitude to share their journey to change lives and a new way of thinking, which helps set the new norm of self-empowering, self-reliance, resilience, and self-discovery.

The mysterious and challenging moments will leave a blueprint for aspiring women across the globe. Countless women across the world will understand that giving up is not an option but to power on is. Is this you or someone you know who went through every trial and tribulation?

Let's not look at her as weak or the situation as her weakness, or if this is you, please don't see yourself as soft. The fact that you have overcome is your power. Every woman and man you know has won their battle; they won because winning is their strength. You overcome every barrier because you are stronger than you ever know.

Keep smiling and shift your energy to love and kindness. Align yourself with positive emotions and create exciting outcomes because it will assist you in finding passion, purpose, and peace to reap the fantastic opportunities with everlasting gratitude for all authenticity, love, equality, and consideration of others. Therefore, only through love can we change a man's heart to bring about peace in our planet's desires. However, if each of us can nurture our heart to accept, forgive, care, understand, get happily for others, and be a servant of wanting the best for others will be the source to overcome trials and tribulations.

Dr. Desziree Richardson is an international, inspirational, and motivational speaker, vibratory voice healer, branding iconic expert, women empowerment advocate, entrepreneur, leader, and humanitarian. Desziree feels a genuine desire and devotion to the wellbeing and welfare of her fellow human beings and appreciates being a service to others. Her work is to reach a broader audience to impact the lives of every human existence. She believes it is one of her sole purposes to share her experience and wisdom to help empower positive changes in many people worldwide.

She is the UK representative for the Birland State government, UK ambassador to United States Presidential Services, an international multicultural distinguished honorary advisor for FOWCAAS.org Singapore, and Ambassador for International Forum for Creativity and Humanity, the Kingdom of Morocco and Safeguarding Children Sava Samiti Agra Uttar Pradesh, India.

Her passion, story, and motivation have helped and inspired others. She has received numerous international awards and recognition for her work, including the Award-Winning World Women Visionary Leader Award, AAA, Humanitarian Award, and the England Gold Award for Leadership and Dedication, Red Blazer of Excellence and Achievement Award, She Rocks Women Empowerment Lifetime Achievement Award, WAW Hall of Fame Honorary Award, Innovative Global Women Empowerment Leadership Award, Woman of Distinguished Existence Titanic Blue Necklace Award, Institution of Global Professionals Women of Influence Award, The Global Empowerment Cheerleader for All Women Award, Outstanding Personality of the Year Award, Woman of Excellence Award, Peace Champion of the Year Award, Lifetime Legend in Leadership Award, Peace Worker Platinum Award, Kutai Mulawarman Education for Peace and Human World Award, Nobility Award, Vessels Social Change, and Impact Award, LMA Motivational Speaker of Year Award and Royal Nobles Heart Award, to name a few.

Desziree uses her voice as an instrument for change and to empower, heal, motivate, and help transform lives into a more fulfilling life of love, kindness, peace, abundance, and acceptance through her accolade of creative projects purposely designed to empower women and uplift humanity. Her sincere transparency has showcased her unique talents as a speaker, author, media personality, broadcaster, and witty reporter. She's authentic, honest, personable, and professional.

As a previous project leader at the University of West London, her leadership and experience involved her managing projects, volunteers, and teams and hosting events in the community, such as planting trees in Gunnersbury Park, interacting with seniors, and creating other community projects that benefit the community and environment and raise funds for Future Sense Charity to support Children in Cambodia.

Desziree also volunteered her time teaching in Asia and completed projects to give back, such as the Sanitary Napkins campaign for young girls in Uganda, holding the first Women of Heart Foundation Golden Awards in Kenya, and projects in Uganda, Liberia, and Nigeria on the ground. She has also helped with fundraising for various charities and hospices across the UK for the Have a Heart Appeal, Help a London Child, The Classic Foundation, and campaigning for the Hunger Summit, IF Enough Food for Everyone, and as a UNICEF Children's Champion.

In addition, she has contributed to many funds and awareness-raising campaigns, including live auction bids with other celebrities, and acted as

Mother Nature, speaking to children at the London Metropolitan University on Climate Change.

Desziree brings a powerful magnetic energy and a uniquc array of women advancement projects to celebrate, motivate, and empower women worldwide. Her empowering media, such as the Women of Heart Awards-WOHA, and Gentlemen of Heart Awards-GOHA, celebrate men and women making a difference in the world. She supports and specializes in women empowerment and appreciates and recognizes men who lift women and the growth of society. Her projects are a great forum to forge connections between like-minded women and men. She believes our world could become more beautiful if everyone thought positively and shared positive energies wherever they go.

Desziree believes as humans, we should all gather our good thoughts and deeds by accepting and welcoming different cultures and religions in the workplace, society, and social norms. As a leader and visionary, her projects sustain, support, and implement diversity and inclusion, which exemplify a sense of belonging that embrace these factors.

Her quote: “Put love in all you do; when love wins, the world wins.”

Website: www.desziree.com

Facebook: Desziree Richardson

Instagram: desziree

About the Visionary Author

International motivational speaker, transformational leader, eight-time bestselling author, three-time international bestselling author, three-time award-winning educator, US Army Veteran, and 28 years in education, Dr. Theresa A. Moseley inspires audiences around the world with her message on peace. Dr. Theresa, also known as "The PeaceMaker," realized at the young age of 14 that one of her gifts was intuition. She uses her unique gift to help others as she has the gift of discernment, and is perceptive. As a child, she always loved to sing and perform on stage and remembers being 2 years old and singing the song Cupid in Augsburg, Germany. When she was 14 and a girl scout, the lights went out at a camporee and her girl scout leader said, "Find Theresa! Tell her to sing." As Theresa sang Ben by Michael Jackson, a hush came over the crowd. All the screaming girl scouts were once again calm listening to Theresa. Her gift is also her voice, and at the time she did not realize that speaking and writing would be how she used her voice to serve the world. Dr. Theresa has a calming presence when she speaks, and her message is loud and clear. Everyone is responsible for making the world a more peaceful place by raising our children to be peaceful. She wrote a book with a Creed at the end for people to become Ambassadors of Peace. Some of her steps include communicating, rather than retaliating, attacking the problem, not the person, cultivating peace by caring, having empathy for others, showing compassion for others, loving your community and serving them well, teaching her family to be peaceful, protest peacefully, and realize your potential and make a difference in the world.

Dr. Theresa has made it her mission to help the world become a more peaceful place after she lost two students and cousins to violence. Dr. Theresa is a virtuous woman and has been recognized internationally for her work in changing the lives of others. Dr. Theresa's next project is her Passion Purpose Peace Academy which will launch in 2023. Her goal is to help people discover self, know their passion, develop a blueprint, monitor progress, network, and have accountability to fulfill their purpose which will lead to inner peace.

Notes...

Notes...

Notes...

Notes...

Notes...

Notes...

Passion Purpose Peace

The Pathway through Trials and Tribulations

Visionary Author Dr. Theresa A. Moseley

Made in the USA
Middletown, DE
10 October 2022

12343781R00076